12 Voices

12 Voices

A Global Coterie Makes
the Case for Cultural Diversity

Mark Bornhoft

Grosbeak
Publishing

ISBN-13: 979-8-218-31022-6
LCCN: 2023920588

Cover design by: John Russo Design
Editor: Steve Bornhoft

I dedicate this book to my parents, who taught me the value of curiosity and learning.

Content

Introduction

Every year our world becomes more complex and diverse. Culture, our guide on how to live together, is falling behind. The slowly evolving collective wisdom of culture isn't keeping up with the accelerated pace of life and our many new decision-points. And with the expanded transparency that most people now experience, we see how neat cultural boxes no longer encompass the intricacy of modern life.

If we can no longer rely on our past collective experience to drive a workable, internalized cultural framework, we run the risk of living without one or relying on external entities such as work, government, social media, or the marketplace to set the standards. That's dangerous because powerful structures tend to set up systems that exploit people.

As these previously accepted paths of life fall short of our expectations, we begin to bear additional responsibility for crafting our own direction. Faced with overwhelming inputs, accelerated change, and expanded options, the task can become insurmountable and lonely — or it can be freeing and rewarding. **As with most dramatic shifts, we face a choice in how to respond.** There is a monumental difference between being threatened by the higher levels of diversity and being enriched by them.

Within this book, you will discover insights that have helped others thrive in this new environment.

I have taken a novel approach to building the book's framework. Franz Boas, the "father of modern anthropology," urged those serious about the study of culture to free themselves from the bonds, bias, and judgement of their own culture.[1] I've strived to reach this lofty goal by using 12 personal, relevant, and diverse global interviews to lay the foundation for moving forward.[2] These narratives from 10 different countries shine a light on the essential elements of the pathway ahead. It's a pathway abounding in diversity.

We are experiencing a deep divide in many places of the world based on seemingly arbitrary parameters: color, country of origin, gender, and class. Many people are lost in a world that surfaces conflicting social signals. My sincere hope is that you will find this book beneficial and enriching in your journey through these challenging times.

---

[1] King, Charles. (2019). *Gods of the Upper Air*. p.247

[2] Interviews are edited for length and clarity. Interviewees were asked to discuss their cultural journey, perceived changes in culture, and the impact of digital transformation.

Part I
Losing our Way in the 21ˢᵗ Century

Chapter 1

Losing our Way

The whole scope ... is to recommend culture as the great help out of our present difficulties; culture being a pursuit of our total perfection by means of getting to know, on all the matters which most concern us, the best which has been thought and said in the world (From preface to *Culture and Anarchy*, Matthew Arnold, 1869)

I have two sons in America, and all they care about in Chinese culture is Jackie Chan and Jet Li. (Ang Lee, Taiwanese filmmaker)[3]

People are born predisposed to behave in certain ways and to satisfy various needs. They all have the will to survive. They have the desire to belong, to build relationships, and to control their destiny. Psychologist Abraham Maslow created a pyramid depicting human's hierarchy of needs. The bottom layer of the pyramid includes physiological and safety needs. In the middle are belongingness, love, and esteem. At the pinnacle is the shared longing for self-realization. With these needs and desires in

---

[3] Ang Lee Quotes. (n.d.). BrainyQuote.com. Retrieved June 24, 2022, from BrainyQuote.com Web site:
https://www.brainyquote.com/quotes/ang_lee_466676

common, people have developed cultures — shared understandings of how to live together. These various cultures reflect the history, geography and other living conditions of regions around the world.

Franz Boas and his supporters believed that culture reflected common sense, the knowledge we use to get along in the world. Culture helps us raise children, resolve conflict, build relationships, and deal with death. Charles King in *Gods of the Upper Air* tracks the achievements of the pioneers of cultural anthropology. He claims that "there is no more fundamental reality in the social world than the one that humans themselves in some measure create."[4]

But the nature of culture is changing. Cultures that took centuries to create, evolve, and refine are crumbling under the weight of current conditions. What if humans are no longer capable of defining a social reality that satisfies human needs in the increasingly complex and diverse world? In such an environment, how do we interact successfully with others? The ramifications for our lives are real.

It could be argued that these cultural changes are for the better. Many people have suffered because of their low cultural status and lack of societal power. Many cultural practices are sexist and racist. Will there soon come a time when the world recognizes the inherent value of all people? I suspect not. The ongoing reshuffling of the deck may well put another group of people at the bottom of the heap.

In many places, the state of life is in such flux that some people are longing for the days when lines were more clearly drawn and stable. This nostalgia is especially prevalent among people who have enjoyed privilege in the past. But even people of modest means may miss the familiar rhythms of life and established pathways to success.

My objective for this book is to provide some tools, examples, and perspectives to welcome diversity, strengthen identity, and take ownership of individual pathways. However, before establishing a new course, it's vital to understand what is happening around us. In the first section of the book, we will explore the current impacts of technology-driven transparency, individual choice, and disruptive change in our lives.

---

[4] King, Charles. (2019). *Gods of the Upper Air*. p.9

Transparency – Think about the impact of the Internet in building awareness of other ways of life in the world. Not only does this give people more ideas about how to live their lives, but it also opens us up to criticism. As of 2020, 4.3 billion of the 7.7 billion people in the world have internet access, and that number is growing.[5]

Individual choice – As countries continue to mature and develop, people have an ever-increasing number of options to follow. As they do, they step outside of established patterns, and act more as an individual.

Disruptive Change – When people experience dramatic change and see instability in their world, they begin to question their fundamental assumptions.

After setting the stage, the heart of this book will present 12 inspiring interviews from people around the globe. By drawing insights from the interviews and expanding on them, we can recognize the importance of our social identities, relationships, and shared pathways. We begin to see how to adapt and move forward.

---

[5] Palgrave Macmillan (Ed.). (2020). *The Statesman s Yearbook 2020: The Politics, Cultures and Economies of the World*

Chapter 2

Culture as a Pathway

As part of our exploration, I'll take you to Iran, Korea, and Southeast Asia to cover cultural transformations. We'll investigate top-down cultures in Thailand, South Korea, Japan, China, and the U.S. You will hear individual voices from many of these countries. Before doing that, I'd like to set the stage and establish some working definitions.

We now live in a continually evolving online world, full of data and influences. Look no further than Google and Facebook (now Meta). Because the data they provide is so influential, they aren't allowed in various countries. In 2019, complete shutdowns of the Internet took place in Hong Kong, Iran, and multiple states in India to deal with internal conflict. Overall, according to research firm Top10VPN, there were 134 intentional shutdowns in 2019 in 21 countries with a total economic cost of over $8 billion. [6] Governments know that access to information changes people. Why else would they block this access even when paying such a high economic price? They are proving my point.

Facebook itself can be a powerful medium. To look at Facebook feeds, you might think that all Facebook friends lead perfect lives. LOL. But

---

[6] Government Internet Shutdowns Have Cost Over $26 Billion Since 2019. *Top10VPN* https://www.top10vpn.com/research/cost-of-internet-shutdowns/

seriously, that's the image that many humans try to project, and it could prove disrupting to countries with people who are beginning to consider their options. Also, people increasingly post politically motivated slogans or news.

Facebook is a cover-up; people don't share negative stuff. I don't believe everything that I hear on Facebook. To learn about someone, who they are, requires meeting in person. Facebook shares too much. Repeating of negative news, such as cop shooting. It is extremely overwhelming. (Laotian voice, Keo)

Perhaps strategies on the part of some countries to limit information make some sense given where they are today. Hear me out. All countries limit or discourage certain types of speech. In the U.S., saying something that is considered racist can lead to you losing your job. Other countries might see that as an abridgment of free speech.

Even our willingness to be open has limitations. There are all sorts of viewpoints and different kinds of people on Facebook, but in the end, people choose their friends, and that determines their information feed. Friends tend to reinforce what people already believe, not to open their minds. The digital revolution also creates soldiers who dance to a different beat. People with dark and destructive tendencies use various digital means to find each other around the world and do harm.

Many around the world have heard of Alibaba. It's one of the top three eCommerce companies in the world with operations in more than 200 countries and headquarters in China. Alibaba has the online malls Taobao, Tmall, Lazada, and AliExpress. Consumers look for bargains there. Their biggest day is Nov. 11, Singles Day, which Alibaba has trademarked as Double 11 (because the date is 11/11). Singles Day started in China as an alternative to Valentine's Day, and eventually Alibaba latched on to it. On this one day, Alibaba online transactions amount to tens of billions of dollars. The key point is transparency. People can see products and pricing from all around the world. There are many large, trans-national companies with a global digital presence, like Amazon, TikTok, and Line.

A few minutes ago, I claimed that information changes us. Let me add to that. **Shared** information changes us even more. As part of one of the interview chapters, I'll take the opportunity to explain the Liquified Life theory. The idea is that making all sorts of information available changes people. For the people who welcome and accept these varied inputs, their lives become more fluid and responsive.

Before I get too deep into our discussion of changes, let's agree on what we mean by "culture." I can always pull out the dictionary definition. Let's do that, as a start. Our first problem is that culture has about 12 meanings at dictionary.com. Let's focus on the two most relevant:

- The behaviors and beliefs characteristic of a particular social, ethnic, or age group: e.g., the youth culture; the drug culture.
- The sum total of ways of living built up by a group of human beings and transmitted from one generation to another.

Based on my own understanding of culture from many global inputs, I suggest the following as our working definition of culture. It resembles number two, above.

Culture is a broadly shared, multi-dimensional roadmap for life that develops as the result of **shared** experiences over **time**, with **common** actions and beliefs being **internalized** as a **response** to **needs** and widely accepted **assumptions**.

Please focus on the bolded words. Culture requires multiple people interacting with stuff they have in common. Over time, that interaction leads to actions and beliefs that they carry inside without even thinking about them.

Why do cultures form? Because people have needs, wants, and fears. Subsequently, they are influenced by others like them who hold the same ideas about how to survive and thrive. Breaking it down further, I would say that culture is:

- Internalized – it is part of our belief system.
- Unconscious – our decisions are influenced by it even in the absence of conscious thought.
- Environmental – our assumptions are a mirror of our ecosystem.
- Self-defining – it forms our identity.

We also talk about the concept of being "multi-cultured." Simply put, being "multi-cultured" means that an individual no longer uses a single broadly shared roadmap to guide his life. The reasons for this are many and we will cover them over the course of this book.

Do you remember times growing up when you felt out of place? You were "one of those things that were not like the others?" Stop, take a minute, and reflect. At that point, did you recognize, maybe for the first time, that you and perhaps your family were somehow different? To me, that's a signal that you had a place where you belonged. You had ideas, beliefs, and standards that you shared with some and not with others. You had the beginnings of a culture.

Looking back on my life, I can isolate two important ways that our family was set apart. The first was a focus on education. Given my father's educational history, it was not surprising. During World War II, my father enlisted in the Marines. The Marines enrolled him in a program to learn radio operations. As he shared with his family, every week or so they would have a test on the material. Those who failed were dropped from the program and sent to the front. My father, using the study methods he so often repeated to us, passed each test, and completed the program. He was then responsible for radio operations on a carrier that was headed to Japan. By the time they arrived, the Japanese had surrendered. Did his study habits save his life? I often thought so. After the war, my father used the GI Bill to earn a degree at the University of Minnesota and apply for a job. He wasn't finished with his educational needs. He accepted a job offer that required a car and a driver's license, neither of which he had. Back to the books to get that license and support his family.

The second way in which my family was different was in the appreciation of nature. As the world was beginning to talk about pollution, the environment, and zero population growth, my parents brought us to a conservation summit in Colorado. I don't remember much about the lectures we attended there, but I vividly remember how excited my parents were when my older brother spotted a bird called a dipper in a stream foraging for food. They were passing that appreciation on to their kids. When I was 10 years old or so, our parents saved enough money to buy a small cabin that we visited each weekend of the summer. We were quite pleased with the long list of birds that we were able to identify there. I remember reading Rachel Carson's *Silent Spring* and Walsh and Robert Gannon's *Time Is Short and the Water Rises, Operation Gwamba*. We were certainly not a flawless model family (more on that later), but we did have some distinguishing characteristics.

The sense of a social identity within a family allows us to consider the relationship between a person and the culture to which they belong. Thomas Turino (2004) states, "social identities are based on recognized similarities within groups, and differences with others, which in turn serve as the basis of collective feeling and action. Group identities are the foundation of all social and political life."[7]

Of course, culture continues to expand and evolve over time, along with your personal and social identities. People incorporate new things as they are exposed to new experiences and ideas.

What are other differences among people? Consider this scenario. People with dissimilar backgrounds get attracted to each other for various reasons, some of which are quite superficial. They make assumptions that they share the same set of values and standards, the same culture. But perhaps they don't.

- "You mean to say that you don't want kids? What is a family without kids?"
- "What's the point of studying and working all the time? I want to enjoy my life."

Remember that I described culture as internalized, unconscious, environmental, and self-defining. Consequently, culture is not something that can be easily altered. It might not respond to logic. In fact, someone might have difficulty explaining the reasons for their position. To them, the position simply makes empirical sense based on their experience and the people closest to them.

Now that we have a working definition of culture, how does the magic happen? How do people acquire a culture? You've acquired one. How did it happen for you?

I suspect that for most people, the process of obtaining a culture happens so slowly that people don't consciously notice it. And a lot of it happens when we are young and impressionable. It's a pathway. If there's

---

[7] Turino, Thomas. (2004). *Identity and the Arts in Diaspora Communities*. p.8

a gap between a person and something they need or want, they take the established pathway, assuming the pathway was created with a purpose. How appropriate that Shari'ah, the name of the code of living for Muslims, means "a way to the watering-place."[8] Buddhism, the fourth largest global religion, also uses the pathway metaphor. The Eightfold Path is the Buddhist guide of practical instructions for improving life.

The implied message of a culture is that the pathway will reliably lead to achievement of your goal. It's a path that was created and improved by a collection of people with similar needs. The path is shared. People use it because they believe it has value, knowing that it has been used by people that they have come to know and trust.

Yes, this is a simplification. There are many different forks in the road taken over time. But culture represents collective wisdom and, at times, a blind faith in following the pathway. A culture helps people make sense of the world.

For another perspective, consider cultural acquisition in Laos, a place we will visit later in our investigations. While in Laos, Hmong families passed along their culture, traditions, and skills orally and by example.[9] In The Spirit Catches You and You Fall Down," Anne Fadiman lists some of the varied and practical Hmong lessons passed to the young, such as how to honor your ancestors, play the qeej, conduct a funeral, court a lover, track a deer, flail a load of rice, and perhaps most importantly, how to grow the opium poppy, their valuable cash crop. The Hmong were mountain people, and opium grows best in the cool environment of higher elevations.[10] These are the lessons of a people, a clan, a family, passed down as culture, traditions, and means of survival.

Let's investigate another example. Imagine two kids, considering their futures. Ideas get planted in their heads even before they recognize them.

- I can see how my parents got ahead. They have it pretty good right now financially. They have a nice house. The way I figure it, education made a big difference. Without it, they wouldn't be able to hold professional jobs. Besides, the way they talk

---

[8] Kamali, Mohammad Hashim. *Shari'ah Law: An Introduction.* p.2
[9] Until recently, there was not a written form of the Hmong language.
[10] Fadiman, A. (1997). *The Spirit Catches You and You Fall Down.* Paperback Edition (2012) p.121

about it, college was a lot of fun. They met some of their best friends at school.

- I can't wait to start working once I get out of high school. My parents have had so many interesting jobs and that's how they've learned about life. Every job taught them something new. I can't believe people spend money they don't have on college and end up in debt. I can't see myself behind a desk.

These are two different paths. Each one is being taken because the family environment demonstrates the way, means, and the end. Each path is familiar and apparently successful.

Of course, it doesn't always work this way. If the kid hates/loves school or the parents hate their jobs, the situation might point in the opposite direction. Regardless, there are actions and ideas that are internalized, unconscious, environmental, and self-defining. And there are all sorts of these over a lifetime. People need to make decisions and cultures supply guidance. Here's an example:

Step 1: **Environmental Change** – Someone is faced with an opportunity, need, or threat. For example, someone heads off to college away from home. The situation is assessed, either consciously or subconsciously: How will I survive? How are other people like me handling this transition? What have I observed in my own experience?

Step 2: **Perceived Benefit (The Value Proposition)** – The perceived benefits of a course of action are assessed through the lenses of culture. This happens almost automatically. The human brain has evolved for thousands of years to enable this. As a young adult, people might already have a cultural framework established; it's just being fine-tuned. A college senior might ask himself, "Where do I want to live the next years of my life? What job should I take? Culture helps determine the answers and provide confidence.

Step 3: **Adoption** – Decisions are made, and actions are taken.

Step 4: **Refinement of Identify** – Identities are altered or reinforced. Others may alter their perceptions of this person.

And so it goes, through the many stages of life. Now that we've moved from a simple path to a whole set of behaviors, allow me to use a different word, "pattern." To me, **a culture is a pattern of actions and ideas** that multiple people share.

Now you know where I stand, and we have a working definition of culture. Throughout history, people have created and adopted cultures to guide their lives collectively and individually. But times have changed. Just ahead, I will present how I see current conditions impacting and altering these processes.

Chapter 3

Modern Day Impacts

In a stable and harmonious world, the adoption of a way of life and a set of guidelines to govern decision-making would be straightforward. After surviving the awkwardness of adolescence, people would confidently interact and build relationships, using universal rules of etiquette. We'd navigate an established course of action — a cow path, if you will — toward common goals. However, for better or worse, that is not the world that most of us experience today.

Often in today's complex society, we either try to restrict our world to comfortable parameters, or we bounce into a multitude of unknowns and shifting expectations. Why? In the next three sections, I'll present three major factors that are changing the social environment we face. It's important that we share an understanding of the current reality before diving into how to deal with it.

Overwhelming Transparency

Transparency is the first of three macro factors that I see impacting the way people understand the world. Transparency comes in many forms:

- It's the revelation that the Founding Fathers that you learned about in high school were far from perfect. (And your high school teachers, too.)
- It's the technology of DNA analysis that frees the innocent on Death Row and calls into question the veracity of the justice system.
- It's behavioral studies that uncover the real reasons people are attracted to each other, succeed, or get depressed.
- It's the exposure to different people and different ways of life that can complement and challenge our own ways of life.

A new level of transparency is enabled by the new digital world. Now there are 3.5 billion Facebook accounts[11] and over a billion WeChat active users. According to a study by IHS Markit Technology, there were 245

---

[11] Palgrave Macmillan (Ed.). (2020). *The Statesman's Yearbook 2020: The Politics, Cultures and Economies of the World*

million video surveillance cameras installed in the world in 2014, which was one camera for every 29 people, and that number is growing.[12] According to Statista, in 2021 there were 6.2 billion smartphone subscriptions in the world.[13] With each of those smartphones, people can take a photo or video and post it to the internet within seconds. People's lives are online. They are living on an entirely different playing field.

Our understanding of the world is changed when new information challenges the foundational assumptions of our belief systems. This can happen when a leader of a movement is discredited due to the exposure of embarrassing personal actions or speech. Or it can happen when science debunks commonly held ideas about the causes of outcomes. Think of how profoundly the recommendations for child rearing have changed over the last 30 years.

Often, people are not adequately prepared to be exposed to reality. What do I mean? Consider celebrities and famous people of the past and present. In the past, with a lack of exposure to reality and the human tendency to categorize, humans were free to fill in the holes and define people. Today, a constant stream of digital content exposing all sides of people's lives can strike a blow to cultural expectations and norms. The belief system is challenged as digital revelations add new color to cultural icons.

Cultures have a map of behavioral expectations that have developed over time and have proven useful. For the reasons we've discussed, people will generally follow those guidelines. But cultures are far from perfect. As we'll learn from the chapters covering various countries, those expectations can be extremely demanding and not compatible with our human nature.

However, as has been demonstrated again and again, cultural transgressions exposed to the public will elicit negative responses. Someone deviates off course, the cultural community protests. The

---

[12] "Video Surveillance: New Installed Base Methodology Yields Revealing Results," IHS Markit, https://ihsmarkit.com/pdf/IHS-Video-surveillance-installed-base(2)_227038110913052132.pdf

[13] "Number of smartphone subscriptions worldwide from 2016 to 2027," statista, https://www.statista.com/statistics/330695/number-of-smartphone-users-worldwide/

cultural norm is reinforced. A degree of conformity to cultural norms is required to allow the system to work as expected. That's how it works within a cohesive cultural community. But with technology, the words and actions are exposed to a wide array of communities and to individuals who have entirely different values.

The negative responses often come from nameless and faceless people (or chatbots) that could belong to any type of community or background. Almost anything that someone says or does may be criticized by someone. These critics may possess different cultural values or could be acting alone out of emotional frustration. The result? A confusing array of negativity that doesn't point in a clear direction. What's more, there is little opportunity for resolution. How many online threads have you seen where people have a meaningful exchange of ideas and resolve their differences?

At an extreme, people or groups who have committed unacceptable behaviors are no longer considered fully human. They face a barrage of online criticism and threats. In Chinese, the phrase for it is 社会性死亡 (shè huì xìng sǐ wáng) or social death.

Live Streaming

Let's look at a related phenomenon that combines some of the elements of transparency that we just discussed. Live streaming has become incredibly popular in China. Through this medium, everyday people have become online celebrities, earning amazing incomes, with some earning over $100,000 a month. What's going on here?

First, let's review the mechanics. It's relatively easy to link a camera to a computer or use a mobile device to stream video on a Chinese social media site such as YY. It's a new level of transparency. Many of these celebrities talk, sing, or dance for their audiences. A lucky few catch the imagination of the viewing public and become a live streaming star. These stars ask their fans to contribute money, which they can do electronically.

Depending on the size of the contribution, some objects (for example, lollipops) will flash across the screen to recognize the gift. By contributing at a certain level, fans achieve status. The celebrity might even mention their name. Many thousands of dollars are given. Some people of very modest means give generously, especially as part of an annual contest to determine the biggest live-streaming star.

Why do people do this? Send money to a person they will never meet? OK, I get it. People have a need to connect. Live streaming also allows someone to see very personal aspects of another person's life. Perhaps giving them money somehow validates the relationship, closes the loop, symbolizes a commitment. Modern life can be very isolating, and a live-streaming relationship can be comforting.

But I'm not here to analyze personal relationships. I'm here to shed light on the effects of transparency. Of course, a particular video streamer may be attractive by virtue of his or her appearance, voice, or personality. I am sure that there are hormones at work here. But along the way, norms are leveraged, and beliefs are influenced.

There are many elements of influence here. It's an intimate, personal, daily look at an extremely likable and popular character. There's no doubt that the streamers evoke cultural norms to build their fan base. As they gain an audience, they can exert influence. How they act and what they believe are powerful drivers due to their perceived success, mass appeal, and personal connection. Through their time and donations, fans are invested.

The live streaming experience is a hybrid connection. In the past, celebrities built their fan base through very controlled and limited exposure that was primarily in only one direction, from the celebrity to the audience. In the digital present, interaction goes both ways and with less control. If there is hope for human culture as a positive force in the future, these intimate and interactive online relationships along with the image-shattering digital revelations must somehow instruct human behavior rather than simply tear apart existing expectations.[14]

Video streamers are sharing their personal lives. Security cameras capture your every move. People are acquiring a mountain of information about others around the world. These are all factors in a new level of transparency that's shaking up shared expectations and assumptions, the building blocks of culture.

---

[14] Do you care to learn more about video streaming? Check out the documentary, *People's Republic of Desire* by Wu Hao. You'll find that, as expected, there's a personal cost to pay for this kind of life and fame.

The way I see it, there are three primary ways in which the new *digital* transparency messes with culture. First, it provides access to many alternative practices and beliefs around the globe that might challenge existing cultural values. Second, the lack of privacy reveals at a personal level that real life often doesn't conform to cultural values, deflating expectations. Third, the preoccupation with online connections outside the core culture-building community interferes with shared experiences and the internalization of a wholistic culture.

Unprecedented Choice

"Cultural adaptation and corporate acceptance of new familial norms is expected. We will most likely see more fractal family units, higher rates of divorces, more focus on career and mobility among younger generations and a greater desire for independency among older generations." (Euromonitor International, 2018)[15]

Under ideal conditions, cultures and identities provide patterns of behavior that help people navigate complicated choices. And in turn, the choices that are made can reinforce and broadcast identities to others. I can see how satisfied and even proud people are when they make decisions (clothes, car, occupation) that fit nicely with their identity and cultural values.

However, the growing number of choices in today's world present a cyclical problem for culture. Culture loses its relevance when it fails to help people navigate an abundance of new choices. As people distance themselves from inadequate cultures, they are less motivated to conform

---

[15] Euromonitor International. (2018). Future of the Family. *Euromonitor International.* Retrieved June 1, 2022 from https://go.euromonitor.com/white-paper-households-2019-future_of_the_family.html

to established patterns, thereby exposing them to even more possibilities. When culture doesn't evolve at a pace to keep up, it becomes irrelevant.

Here's an example. Increasingly, teenagers in various locales are now faced with a decision on their own sexual identity. Gender is no longer considered fixed or binary. It is possible to alter one's physical characteristics and assume a new gender. How many mainstream cultures have accounted for this choice?

As teenagers become young adults, they face another challenging decision, their occupation. Obviously, these options have expanded greatly over the last 200 years. I found a list of common occupations in 1800.[16] There were 23 of them. Before electricity became commonplace, a lamp oil salesman would go door to door. A rag picker was a person who hunted for items to sell for reuse. Want to guess how many occupations are included by the U.S. Bureau of Labor Statistics in the Occupational Employment Wage Statistics? There were 832 in 2021.[17] And by the way, careerplanner.com has a list of 1,388 careers and over 12,000 job descriptions/titles.[18] Finally, career changes in the modern era provide additional options and disruptions. In a study of the U.S. Bureau of Labor Statistics, individuals born from 1957-64 held an average of 12.4 jobs from ages 18 to 54.[19] That's a long way from the formerly established process of inheriting your parent's occupation.

Divorce is another disrupter. The idea that one may choose divorce for a variety of personal reasons has expanded over time. Once someone has departed from the course of "until death do us part," they are more likely to challenge other established ideas, sometimes out of necessity. A divorced spouse may need to take up an entirely new occupation simply to survive. Internationally the proportion of adults aged 35-39 who are

---

[16] "Most Common Jobs in the 1800s. (2021, Sep). "Working the Flame, https://workingtheflame.com/common-jobs-in-the-1800s/

[17] "Occupational Employment and Wage Statistics," (2022, March) U.S. Bureau of Labor Statistics, https://www.bls.gov/oes/,

[18] "List of 12,000 Careers," Career Planner, https://www.careerplanner.com/ListOfCareers.cfm

[19] Bureau of Labor Statistics, U.S. Department of Labor (2021, August 31) https://www.bls.gov/news.release/pdf/nlsoy.pdf

divorced or separated doubled from 1970 to the 2000's.[20] Still, I would argue that many cultures do not offer much support in terms of navigation through a divorce. Rather, divorce is often considered a disappointment that people must face, often on their own. In Singapore, divorced people, as well as unmarried and widowed parents, are considered by the state to be unfortunate and unhealthy.[21]

Faced with increasing levels of choice, are people so knowledgeable, so confident, and so independent that they are willing to forsake shared understandings and established patterns of behavior on a large scale? Can they make decisions on a widening set of choices on their own terms and not based on established pathways? Do they form an identity on their own rather than as part of a community?

Today's reality provides a dilemma. Cultures serve people, partly because they help people deal with a complex world. But if the world is extremely complex and constantly changing, with many choices and decisions to be made, the mapping of the human experience to desirable outcomes becomes extremely difficult.

Consider yourself the master planner of society in a place like the U.S. How do you build a workable culture in a place where so many choices and behaviors exist? If a culture is an established pattern of behavior, there are simply too many possibilities to weave into a recognizable and consistent form.

Later, I will discuss the concept of cultural vectors, the idea that values are directional and unlimited. "Choice" is one of those cultural vectors in many places of the world, particularly in the United States. Many people believe that the more choices, the better. People like the notion that a person can grow up and become anything. People walk down the grocery aisle and choose among a hundred different variations of water, juices, and soda.

---

[20] "Population Facts", (2011, Dec) United Nations, https://www.un.org/en/development/desa/population/publications/pdf/popfacts/PopFacts_2011-1.pdf,

[21] Wong, Theresa, Yeoh, Brenda S. A., Graham, Elspeth F. & Teo, Peggy. (2004, January/February). Spaces of silence: single parenthood and the 'normal family' in Singapore. *Population, Space, and Place*, Volume10, Issue1. Pages 43-58

Let's talk about political scandal. In 1972–1974, the Watergate scandal involved the coverup of election-related dirty tricks of the Nixon administration. On Jan. 6, 2021, supporters of Trump violently broke into the U.S. Capitol. The subsequent investigations of each scandal were televised. At the time of Watergate, there existed three major television networks and the public broadcasting system (PBS). All these stations carried live televised proceedings of the investigation. At the time of these Watergate hearings, a television viewer had no choice other than to watch the proceedings. Not so in 2022. As with Watergate, the Jan. 6 investigation was covered by multiple networks. However, people in 2022 also had a wide array of other media choices viewable on a variety of devices. For the Watergate scandal in the 1970s, people were funneled into a common viewing experience that led to over-the-fence or water-cooler discussion. But in 2022, people were free to choose from a wide variety of perspectives or digital entertainment alternatives.

People make choices based on personal preferences and inherited dispositions. They are influenced by a wealth of information and marketing. They are pursuing happiness, as the U.S. Constitution and other country frameworks would have them do. But in the process, people have abandoned some of the benefits of culture.

People are not self-sufficient, independent, and emotionally strong "out of the box." Most birds have a couple of weeks or less before they are coaxed or pushed out of the nest. In contrast, humans are raised by parents for years in a complex process of learning and maturing. It's not an easy job and, unfortunately, many people embark upon adulthood with significant gaps and issues.

The way I see it, the major benefits of a culture can be grouped into two categories. On the one hand, cultures justify and make sense of constraints imposed by human limitations, governments, and industry. In other words, they help people deal with imperfect environments and the realities of life. The discrepancy between human needs and the lives they lead necessitates a culture. Cultures help people through 12-hour workdays by elevating the shared value of a work ethic. They help people deal with the death of a loved one via rituals and structured community interaction. On the other hand, cultures provide a proactive roadmap of how to live a rewarding human life. For example, various cultures promote education, respect for elders, and long-term goals.

Think of it this way: Cultures provide both defensive benefit (preserving order and a psychological framework) and offensive benefit (guiding constructive decision-making). As the world becomes more complicated and information undermines superstition, cultures will need to operate at higher, more generalized levels to be relevant. Cultures can't afford to set fixed and constrained patterns because in a world of increased choice, those detailed patterns are no longer practical.

Consider an example from rural China. In the December 2019 issue of *News China*, there was a report on a village ban on funeral gowns. Apparently, many places in rural China have a practice that all children of the deceased must wear white linen mourning gowns. Authorities in a village in Xiangfen County, Shanxi Province, decided it would be a good idea to move away from this custom by banning it and punishing the families who violated the ban. The children of violators would become ineligible for residence permits and education.

What a dilemma. The authorities felt that the practice was superstitious and generated wasteful spending. Yet many people reacted strongly to the ban. Many villagers and online voices considered it illegal for the government to deny children education and wrong to disrespect local customs.

Basically, it's an issue of choice, wouldn't you agree? The local custom demands conformity with the practice. The local authorities, applying what they would consider practical modern thinking, ban the practice. Applying the now widely adopted principle of choice, most people felt villagers should be able to decide on their own. That's the way the world is headed, away from fixed cultural expectations and toward a format that accommodates a new environment of choice.

Choice itself can be demanding. I suspect that in this new environment, a certain percentage of people will be overwhelmed. Without the safety net of a viable culture, psychological issues such as mental illness and suicide could climb.

Here's an example from North Korea to prove my point. There, the state defines reality and tells people what is right and wrong. It demands conformity. Because of tight controls and isolation, people lack the information and ability to make intelligent and informed decisions. Every year, people risk their life to escape North Korea. For those who make it to South Korea, you might think that they are eager and happy to begin a life of freedom and choice. Experience has shown otherwise.

After a long process of being cleared by South Korean national security at the National Intelligence Center, escapees from North Korea are sent to a resettlement center. The Hanawon resettlement center is about 40 miles south of Seoul. It was built in 1999 to handle the mass transitioning of people that would result if North and South Korea were unified. In the center, escapees from North Korea are taught how to make decisions, something they have little experience doing. Just as North Koreans are overwhelmed by the choices they find in South Korea, many others around the world need help to navigate the complex sets of choices that they now face.

Disruptive Change

As they search for new values against the uncertainties of the present and the debunking of the past, many young people today refuse to believe that, without the contributions of their grandparents and great-grandparents, the confident, modernizing China they now know would not exist. (Xue Xinran, *China Witness*)

The number of people crossing borders is growing. Maybe because of social media, transportation, and globalization, the world is shrinking and people from different cultures are going to have to learn how to live with each other. (Dr. Kemal Kirisci, Senior Fellow, Brookings Institution, from the documentary, *Human Flow*, an Amazon Studios film by Ai Weiwei)

There is an increasing amount of instability in the world today due to disruptive change. It is the last of the three major factors that I see impacting traditional culture.

One might think that with all the technological advances in the most advanced countries of the world, there would be an unprecedented amount of stability in a place like the U.S. To some degree that is true.

However, the linchpin which is the family is suffering. The percentage of U.S. children living with an unmarried parent more than doubled over a period of only 49 years, climbing from 13% in 1968 to 32% in 2017. For that same period, the following statistic is even more disturbing. It is estimated that by the time a child reaches 9, more than 20% of those born to a married couple and over 50% born to a cohabiting couple will experience the breakup of their parents.

What do adults have to say about these trends? In a 2015 survey, two-thirds of adults said that an increase in single women raising children on their own was bad for society, and 48% said the same about more unmarried couples raising children.[22]

Sounds like something very basic is broken. Either the cultural standards are out of date, conditions are challenging, or the support for the cultural ideals is lacking. Or perhaps all three. Regardless, many people are making key life decisions to handle their individual needs, not to satisfy a cultural standard. And who can blame them? What benefit does membership in a group provide when it rejects their way of life?

Speaking of families, it's time I brought up a concept that was promulgated in the U.S. in the 1960s, the generation gap. The term referred to the stark differences between the youthful baby boom generation and the generation that raised them in areas including politics, lifestyles, morals and mores, dress, and music. The collective ideas and lifestyle changes promoted and practiced by the new generation were labeled as a counterculture. This phenomenon is not unique to the United States. In China, the accomplished author Xue Xinran interviewed a wide variety of people who had lived through the Cultural Revolution. While the people interviewed held very different occupations and positions in the social hierarchy, their experiences with the younger generations were very similar. The interviewees shared how the younger generation was not interested in the sacrifices of the older generation and dismissed them for their loyalty to the now outmoded revolutionary ideals.[23]

---

[22] Statistics on families are based on the U.S. Census and on analysis and surveys by Pew Research https://www.pewresearch.org/social-trends/2018/04/25/the-changing-profile-of-unmarried-parents/
[23] Xue, Xinran. (2009). *China Witness*

While these generational gaps are not new, they are clearly disruptive. With each generational turnover, there is the potential, and I would say likelihood, for lifestyles to become individualized.

Consider an indigenous people, the Ojibwe. Due to the loss of land and forced assimilation, Ojibwe culture has been lost. Each new generation needs to be convinced that the work of acquiring the rich culture and language of the Ojibwe is worth the effort. It is no simple task. Anton Treuer, a Princeton University graduate, gave up his career aspirations to recapture and teach traditional Ojibwe living. He was fortunate to work with the chief of one of seven active medicine dance lodges. Treuer writes about the challenging process of learning the many Ojibwe cultures. Many cultural practices must be practiced and handed down in person. In fact, there are taboos about what can be shared in book form or with mixed company.[24]

Let's turn our attention to another destabilizing trend. Our world is now experiencing the highest levels of displacement on record according to the UNHCR, the United Nations Refugee Agency. At the end of 2021, there were an estimated 89.3 million displaced people. This is the highest number since World War II. Of that 89.3M, 53.2M are internally displaced, 27.1M are refugees, 4.6M are asylum-seekers and 4.4M are Venezuelans displaced abroad. More than two thirds of the refugees come from five countries: Syrian Arab Republic, Venezuela, Afghanistan, South Sudan, and Myanmar.[25]

Need we discuss how disruptive displacement can be? The loss of a job and social status is almost guaranteed. People struggle with housing, employment, new languages, and different customs and values. Over time, parents can become dependent on their own children who pick up valuable local knowledge and practical skills in school.

If a culture is an internalized pattern of behavior that works for a collection of people, how will that pattern of behavior succeed when groups of people are moved to a new place with different values and resources? Cultures are crafted based on an ecosystem. They depend on

---

[24] Treuer, Anton. (2021). *The Cultural Toolbox: Traditional Ojibwe Living in the Modern World.* p.11

[25] Global Trends Report 2021 (June 2022) *UNHCR The UN Refugee Agency*
https://www.unhcr.org/about-unhcr/who-we-are/figures-glance

commonly available resources, which are likely very different in a new place. In a culture, people fill roles, and they depend on others to play their respective supporting roles. For displaced people, that balance has been upset, and they are often without solid financial resources.

I realize that humans can be very resilient and resourceful. The will to survive and to protect your family is a primal force. People find a way to carry on, and I admire that. People will band together in small communities and try to reconstruct a life that makes sense to them. To survive is one thing, but people need more. As stated by a displaced woman, "Peace must return. We want our rights, our identity, our language, that's what we want."[26]

People and cultures can adapt, but only to a certain point. Adults with internalized cultures won't completely lose the values, vectors, and beliefs within them. But compromises are made, and some degree of assimilation becomes essential.

Consider the impacts on the host country. Currently, the five main countries for asylum of refugees are Turkey, Pakistan, Uganda, Sudan and Germany. At a minimum, there will be misunderstandings as people of different cultures live out their lives using different playbooks and belief system. When resources are strained, conflicts between host and refugee populations are likely.

Conditions in Syria demonstrate another cruel dimension of displacement. When the Syrian regime laid siege to the province of Idlib in early 2020, about half of Idlib already consisted of displaced Syrians. For some there, they will be forced to run for their lives for the second, third or fourth time.

Germany is hosting about 1.1M refugees, which is about 1.3% of their population. One might think that 1.3% is a relatively small percentage, but many people in Germany are upset about the influx. They are not alone. In 2018, there were 74 border walls with 15 others in some stage of planning across the world.[27] Even though resistance to refugees is

---

[26] Human Flow, an Amazon Studios film by Ai Weiwei, 2017

[27] Vallet, Elisabeth. (2022, March 2). The World Is Witnessing a Rapid Proliferation of Border Walls. *Migration Policy Institute.* https://www.migrationpolicy.org/article/rapid-proliferation-number-border-walls

growing, the displacement continues as strong forces drive people to seek safety, shelter, food and water.

It seems that humans haven't yet developed an effective means to mediate cultural differences. Cultures take time to evolve and merge. It's a power struggle with both identity and livelihood at stake. Yuval Noah Harari, author of best-selling book, *Sapiens: A Brief History of Humankind*, raises the question, "At present, it is far from clear whether Europe can find a middle path that will enable it to keep its gates open to strangers without being destabilized by people who don't share its values."[28]

Consider the fact that refugees worldwide spend an average of 26 years displaced from their homes.[29] This is a harsh reality. In those 26 years, a new generation is born and grows up, not knowing the homeland. This new generation often sees more value in learning the language and customs of the land they occupy than of a land they've never known. For example, in *The Geopolitics of Emotion*, Dominique Moisi states that about 40% of European Muslims are marrying outside of their community of origin.[30] What kind of a culture do displaced people acquire? Are they allowed to assimilate into their adopted place of residence? Can they return to their homeland as complete members? What culture do they teach their children?

We've been focusing on refugees. How about immigrants overall (which includes refugees)? There are almost 50M immigrants living in the U.S. as of 2017. That's around 14% of the U.S. population, which is nearly triple the percentage (4.8) in 1970. One in five people in Canada (22%) are foreign born, and in Australia, it's nearly three-in-ten people (28%).[31]

Based on what we are seeing, the increased movement of people around the world, whether forced or not, will have a significant impact on how we interact. In the best-case scenario, this interaction of displaced and resident peoples will eventually result in a new level of diversity, with both sides making accommodations. The reality of accelerated mobility

---

[28] Harari, Yuval Noah. (2018). *21 Lessons for the 21st Century*. p.156

[29] Ai Weiwei (Director). (2017). *Human Flow* [Film]

[30] Moisi, Dominique. (2010). *The Geopolitics of Emotion: How Cultures of Fear, Humiliation, and Hope are reshaping the World*

[31] Statistics on immigrants are sourced from the United Nations and analyzed by Pew Research, https://www.pewresearch.org/global/interactives/global-migrant-stocks-map/

together with the availability of choice and the increased transparency of a networked world will encourage people to act independently, motivated by expediency and self-interest.

We are almost done covering the modern impacts to culture, and it might seem overwhelming. In the following chapters, you'll find examples of how people have survived and thrived. In the chapter on the Hmong experience, you'll learn how this group of people has adjusted through multiple displacements.

Other Mobility

Apart from displacement, people often move voluntarily. Even though these moves are less disruptive, they still complicate a person's circumstances. And voluntary moves are much more frequent and larger in scope. According to the U.S. Census Bureau, the average person in the U.S. moves more than 11 times in his lifetime. In 2017-2018, a little more than 12% of children of ages 5 to 9 moved, a sensitive time of life for cultural development in children.

A Gallup Poll from 2013 found that about 25% of U.S. adults had moved within the country in the last five years. Moves in Europe are somewhat less frequent. Some European countries have a five-year rate as low as 6-10%, while Finland and Norway are above 20%. Australia is 16-20% and Brazil, 11-15%.[32]

One of the reasons people willingly move to another country is to find a better job. At the end of 2021, about 560,000 Vietnamese people were working in more than 43 countries and territories worldwide, according to statistics published by the *International Labour Organization*. In 2019, 152,530 laborers left Vietnam to work abroad, surpassing the department's plan for 2019 by 27.1%.[33] Imagine people from Vietnam uprooting themselves and moving to unfamiliar places like Japan, Taiwan,

---

[32] Esipova, N., Pugliese, A., & Ray, J. (2013, May 15). 381 Million Adults Worldwide Migrate Within Countries. *Gallup*. https://news.gallup.com/poll/162488/381-million-adults-worldwide-migrate-within-countries.aspx

[33] TRIANGLE in ASEAN Quarterly Briefing Note. (2021). *International Labour Organization*. https://www.ilo.org/wcmsp5/groups/public/---asia/---ro-bangkok/documents/genericdocument/wcms_735109.pdf

the Republic of Korea, Romania and Saudi Arabia. No doubt their worldview will be changed as a result.

One must also consider the dramatic increase in global travel. The number of international tourist arrivals worldwide went from 25M in 1950 to a hefty 1,465M in 2019.[34] That's almost 60 times higher. International travel exposes people to new ideas and relationships, which can have a dramatic effect, especially for people who have lived for generations in isolation. The pandemic caused a dramatic reduction in international travel, but consider that it was international travel that allowed COVID and its many variants to spread quickly around the world. Disruptive ideas can travel just as fast.

Another factor in mobility is international students. The U.S. hosts more international students than any other country. An extended stay in any country for advanced education allows for an even greater influence on the student, his family, and classmates. According to Open Doors (2018), there were 1.09 million international students in the U.S., a 1.5% increase over the previous year.[35]

My point is that mobility, whether through displacement, disruption, or choice, exposes people to new conditions and relationships and requires new approaches for survival and success. This situation will invariably influence the development of culture in youth and the strength of established culture in adults. The global increases in mobility are across the board in terms of displaced persons, voluntary moves, international travel and foreign students. It's inevitable that this acceleration of diverse connections will affect societal development. I believe that it will take some proactive management to maximize the benefit of this diversity and handle the potential issues.

Time to summarize some of the disruptive changes we've considered. See the table below. I've included my thinking on the potential impact to people's cultural framework.

---

[34] Number of international tourist arrivals worldwide from 1950 to 2021 (2022) *Statista*. https://news.gallup.com/poll/162488/381-million-adults-worldwide-migrate-within-countries.aspx

[35] Open Doors. (2018). 2018 Open Doors Report on International Educational Exchange. Institute of International Education and U.S. Department of State's Bureau of Educational and Cultural Affairs

Disruptive change	Potential Impact to Cultural Framework
Generational turnover	Allows the new generation to redefine what culture means to them.
Increased levels of divorce	Questions a foundational element of most cultures, marriage; often requires lifestyle changes
Breakups of parental figures in the first 9 years of life	Loss, change, and inconsistencies in parental examples and teaching
Global Pandemic	Loss of faith in the ability of institutions and people to keep the world safe.
Relocation due to war or threats to safety	Loss of status, employment, resources, family, and support system
Relocation for economic improvement	Exposure to new lifestyles and pathways to success
Climate change	The climate crisis calls into question the current levels of production and consumption. It calls for immediate and extraordinary change
Political polarization	Internalizing and defending extreme positions is psychologically burdensome.

Some degree of stability is vital to the creation and sustenance of our frameworks. For the reasons we've discussed, the disruptive changes that we have covered are altering the established patterns of cultural adoption and retention, which complicates our cross-cultural relationships. Complicates, yes, but often enriches them as well.

The nature of culture might be changing, but our personal needs for identity, relationships and guidance remain the same. Through the upcoming interviews, we take a deeper dive into those needs. In the process, you'll gain wisdom and experience from people around the world.

Part II
Global Insights Light the Pathway Forward

Overview of Global Interviews

The message of Part I of this book, simply stated, is that we rely on cultural and other pathways to make sense of the world, guide our decisions, and form our identities. Furthermore, these pathways have recently been shaken by profound conditions in the world.

Given this turmoil and the demands we face, I sense a need to re-examine our human nature and rebalance our cultural foundations. I believe that we all share common human characteristics that inform our needs in this regard.

In Part II, we turn to the collective wisdom of human experience. I have been extremely fortunate to connect with many insightful people around the world. This section presents 12 global interviews that provide diverse, intimate insights. I'll be using the interviews as a springboard for reflections on managing the new environment. The goal is to capture the collective wisdom of these diverse voices so that they can be distilled into a dynamic model.

Following each interview, in one or more chapters, I will build on the theme that the interview introduces and provide evidence and analysis to back up the conclusions. In doing so, I will share cultural transformations in Iran, Korea, and the Hmong diaspora. Insights from social phenomenon such as K-Pop, online dating apps, and royalty are also provided.

The interviews show how people in a wide variety of circumstances are successfully making their way. The interview themes provide a reminder of how humans operate. They illuminate the core moving parts of our human nature that must be considered as we form our personal world view and interact with others outside of our immediate domain.

I am not asking people to dismiss the cultural elements that work for them. What I am suggesting is that we build our own individual pathways with an awareness of our endowed human nature and the diverse pathways followed by others.

Chapter 4

People seek their Place in the World
Russian Voice

In this interview, you'll hear from a lively and spirited woman from Russia. You will learn how much the opening up of Russia meant to her. She values Russia's cultural past, but has an immense hunger to know and find her place in the outside world. She presents an example of how newfound transparency and options can alter perceptions and cultural identity.

Name: Есения (Eseniia)

Self-description: Happy person, digital practitioner, goal-oriented (Born and raised in Russia and living in Poland. Interview in 2016 with an update from May 2020.)

Cultural Interaction

The fact that we were isolated made us more traditional. I like that. I appreciate how until now we keep our culture. It is important to keep your culture, to take some good from international, but keep celebrating your holidays, and eat the special foods. After 2005, things begin to change significantly in Russia.

I have been traveling for 11 years and have traveled to 22 countries. My first big trip was to the U.S., even though it was difficult back then. I start to be more open. In my country, we only have white people. Russians still watch international people like they are from another planet. They watch every piece of their body. It is not that they don't trust them, but they are curious. They watch to understand and accept a different culture.

I don't think that the cultures give you something different, it is the different character of the individual. When I travel, I find my soul mates. I have trouble finding such people in my country, people that are similar to me in my mind. I now believe that some people have a destiny to travel because all their soul mates are abroad.

I come back from my travels a little bit different. I want to come back to the life I had in my travels. Sometimes I don't want to talk with my friends. I want to spend a few days alone. We can be different people on our travels and be free to think clearly.

My English is so good when I am in the U.S. I start to think in English. It changes the logic of my mind. When I think in English and when I think in Russian, I think differently. It helps me in my work. People in the U.S. think more simply, more clearly. It takes time to understand why people think differently. When I just came to [my job], they encourage people to accept others. I needed to think about what I was saying and how people were seeing me.

Digital Influence

I still remember my first computer in 2007. When I came back home for my birthday party, my parents had a computer for me. My parents bought it for me, and they kept it for almost 10 years. For me personally, it is more important to have a connection in real life. Not just digital all the time. You can't feel what they feel in digital. There is no emotional connection in many cases. We build a relationship on emotional connections. Digital is good to supplement a relationship.

Digital is more negative because of the news and because of my attitude for some of the events. I post my picture in Facebook and one of my friends didn't 'like' it. I didn't know if he didn't like because he didn't see it or was on vacation. It gives me a bad feeling. It is important to filter what you see in the digital world. I don't watch TV in my home. I really want to filter it out because it really affects me. You feel sad without any normal reasons for it.

Update (May 2020)

Since this interview was taken, I moved to Poland and my life completely changed from many perspectives: I deep dive into Polish culture, start to learn Polish language, tried different parts of digital and found myself in digital campaigns. I think it's just coincidence, but I found myself in another country and continue this happy journey.

Nowadays I have mix of traditions I follow (Russian and Polish), I love them both and it's good to have this choice. I love to discover cultures and digital helps me to do it anywhere, anytime and in depth.

My Observations and Reflections

Eseniia embodies global cultural changes. As Russia opened, she welcomed the increased transparency and took opportunities to immerse herself in the newly available diversity. She finds her soulmates outside rather than inside of her homeland. With her extended stay in Poland, she moves beyond a traditional Russian culture to a new mix of traditions. Some might say that this adoption of new cultural values means a corresponding loss of existing culture. I don't agree. However, I do believe that the adoption of a new cultural value outside of your traditional culture does lead to a more complicated and individualized cultural fingerprint, which has implications of isolation. What influences your adoption of new values? Must they be time-tested, approved by your significant others, and part of your ancestral heritage?

In my youth, my experience with Russian culture consisted of history books, news reports, and cartoon characters. Russia was represented as a fearful competitor to the United States. Boris and Natasha were the cartoon Russian spies. On my Aeroflot flight from Istanbul to Moscow for my first work visit there, I chatted with someone that I imagined to be the daughter of a rich oligarch. She was traveling from her family's vacation home in Turkey back to Russia. After engaging her in conversation, I saw her nod to someone I assumed to be her bodyguard, indicating that I was not a threat. He nodded in reply. I was caught up in my Russian stereotypes.

As part of my preparation for the trip, I read about dealing with Russian culture. I was warned to expect many nyet's (no's). Instead, our work group was relieved to be greeted warmly and enjoyed a boat ride on the Moscow River. As Eseniia noted, Russians are very eager to learn more about foreigners. While interesting and insightful, my visits to Russia were not enough to form a substantial picture of typical Russian cultural beliefs. Does such a standard even exist? I don't know. I do believe that many people there are in cultural transition. Think of the political turbulence they have endured in the last 50 years.

If art reflects culture, perhaps my most surprising cultural encounter was the set of bronze sculptures called "Children are the Victims of Adult Vices." One evening on a long, chilly walk in Moscow guided by our Russian colleague, we arrived at a sculpture park. This was not a collection of Russian war heroes. The statues represented destructive conditions that adults inflict upon children. The images of that dark winter evening were unsettling. Child labor was depicted as a factory owner with the head of a bird. Poverty was depicted as an old woman begging for alms. Drug addiction was a man with bent wings offering a syringe. Other vices included prostitution, ignorance, violence, and war. Though they were disturbing, I take comfort in retrospect knowing that Muscovites recognize the preciousness of children and the wrongness of these conditions. Universal cultural values, perhaps?

What have I learned from Eseniia? She opened my eyes to the expansiveness of Russian identities and ideas. As an energetic, intelligent, and optimistic woman, she motivates others. But my biggest takeaway is her desire to seek her place in the world. With the opening of Russia, Eseniia traveled to 22 different countries, many times on her own. She, like other Russians, watches foreigners closely to understand them. She seeks her soulmates. Having been isolated for so long, she longs to see how she relates to others. To me, it sounds like Eseniia is still searching for her cultural home.

Eseniia has revealed the first of the themes, a role for culture to facilitate: **People seek their place in the world.** When someone is comfortable with how they relate to others, that sense of place is reassuring.

One might think that modern communication technology would facilitate this process of clarifying cultural positions. Instead, the technology tends to redraw and blur the lines. The next section, "The Net Effect," explains how.

The Net Effect

Some values are changing, because, for example, your mom and dad are not the people that know the most, your uncle or aunty is not the person that knows the most, Google knows the most. (Iranian voice,ساق)

Even though we are in Thailand, we can know about what happened in other countries. The biggest change for the next generation is that they live in the new digital world. (Thai voice, สุจินดา)

Ever heard of Coolie's looking-glass theory? It's the idea that we learn about ourselves based on how others react to us. Analyzing responses by people to situations helps us understand what is going on outside of our confined existence.

One of the best ways to do this is to study what goes viral. Obviously, if thousands or millions of people show an interest in something, whether it's on Facebook, YouTube, VKontakte, or WeChat, it's important in some way. I have cataloged a few of the common trends. Let's start with an easy one, cat and dog videos. Apparently, people can't get enough of them.

With an abundance of data, I have reached some conclusions. If something is small, furry, and seemingly harmless, anything it does is highly valued. Also, humans will freely interpret cat or dog activity in terms of their own mental framework. People, me included, believe their pets love, talk, feel jealousy, and have deep thoughts, a striking example of anthropomorphism.

But let's expand our horizon and check out some viral activity in China taken from a periodical called *News China*. I am going to challenge you to predict some human reactions. Each of these scenarios elicited a viral reaction, which I'll ask you to guess.

Situation: In China, intense competition at schools produces lots of stress. So, it might not be too surprising to find that on a spring day in Chongqing, more than 2,000 university students engaged in a watermelon fight. They hurled chunks of watermelon at each other for about an hour and went through more than one ton of the fruit.[36]

What do you think the general online reaction was?
- They gave praise to the university regarding this novel idea for relieving stress. Applications to the university went up.
- The event was considered wasteful, and people asked who took responsibility for cleaning it up.
- Many other students publicized similar events held at their university and supported the use of these stress-relievers.
- People did not believe the story was true.

Here's one more question, and it's about love.

Situation: A love story about two high achieving students at Southeastern University in China was posted online. The couple has

---

[36] News China. (Aug 2016). Netizenwatch: Watermelon Warriors. *China Newsweek Corporation*

combined to win 36 awards, and they have published multiple papers. However, many Chinese schools discourage dating between classmates.[37]

In this case, what do you think was the prevailing viral reaction to the love story?

- Readers called for the recall of their top awards and said they should be given to more deserving, unattached students.
- The students were accused of cheating together. How else could they do so well while maintaining a relationship?
- They were encouraged to marry and have a baby, who, undoubtedly, would be very smart.
- Both students were held up as successful examples of balancing schoolwork and romance.

(Read on. The answers are at the end of this chapter.)

Many people flock to viral activity. It's human nature. They are curious about what is going on. They experience FOMO, the fear of missing out. So, they check things out and react. But, trust me, something else is going on.

People are reacting, but they are also learning. Most humans think that they have finely defined operating principles and a clear fixed opinion on things. I don't agree. We often change our minds. When we see and read a viral reaction, we assess the opinion of the masses through a prism that includes our core beliefs, experiences, and emotions. We might reassess our place in the world. Here is where I am impressed with the processing power of the human brain.

A mass of a million people will pull some weight in the human psyche. As you are aware, with modern technology and social media, people can now easily consume the very personal thoughts, experiences, and opinions of a diverse population and factor them into their lives. Inevitably, this transparency impacts stagnant cultures because it greatly expands and accelerates conflicting input and/or fresh ideas. I call this the "net effect."

---

[37] News China. (Aug 2016). Netizenwatch: Nerd Lovers. *China Newsweek Corporation*

This speed of group adaptation through the net effect can be demonstrated by something that has recently gone global, Halloween. The observance started with the Celts, who 2000 years ago lived where Ireland is today. Their year began on Nov. 1 and Oct. 31 was a day of ghosts and prophesies. Celts built bonfires and put on masks.

Then the Romans conquered the Celts and changed things up a bit. The Christian church got into the mix and created All Martyrs Day and eventually All Souls Day. It seems they wanted to replace the Celtic celebration with something that was church-sanctioned.

People from Europe, especially the Irish, helped create a new variation when they emigrated to America. That's when people started dressing up and going door to door.

My point is that all those changes took centuries. Now Halloween is going global in a matter of a few years. Take Japan for example. The Japanese have recently embraced Halloween and made some adaptations, which continue to evolve. It's a good fit, given Japan's obsession with cosplay, the practice of wearing costumes to portray fictional characters. Prior to 2000 in Japan, Halloween was mostly for foreigners, with parties held in the subway. Now, the Kawasaki Halloween Parade is one of many street celebrations in Japan. In 2018, there were about 4,000 costumed celebrants with over 100,000 watching.[38]

Adaptations will continue to occur at an accelerated pace. People see pictures, hear stories, and watch videos of Halloween parties with folks dressed up and eating candy. What's not to like?

Of all the holidays in the U.S., Halloween is the second biggest one for spend. About a quarter of the candy purchased in the U.S. in a year is for Halloween. No doubt commercial success is a factor in the sustainability of a custom. It's worth noting at this point that the Halloween of today is less an integrated cultural tradition than a superficial representation.

Anyway, back to my point. Cultures adapt, evolve and homogenize when they intersect. The net effect speeds change considerably. Halloween proves my point. Christmas is another. There are people around the world celebrating Christmas who aren't Christian. Although there are few Christians in Thailand, many Thai celebrate Christmas with

---

[38] "Kawasaki Halloween Parade" GaijinPot, https://travel.gaijinpot.com/kawasaki-halloween-parade/

a meal, decorations, and gift exchanges. [39] Travel around Asia in December, and you'll see many artificial Christmas trees with festive decorations.

The net effect can also break down existing cultural beliefs and practices. Consider patriotism. Certain societal structures demand conformity with this ideal. They appeal for support through emotional messaging. The net effect allows contrary ideas to reach broadly into the population. As a result, perceived weaknesses of the ideal are exposed and like-minded people share their own concerns. For some, the cultural ideal suffers a very visible black eye and the cycle of resistance gains steam.

The ease of finding and spreading electronic information isn't the first dramatic change in information exchange. Distribution of the printed word democratized the availability of information and spread public opinion. The printed word allowed Martin Luther's criticism of the Catholic church to be distributed. His translation and printing of the Bible put the sacred text into the hands of believers and shaped their own faith. The Lutheran church was born. Condemnation of the nobility and their transgressions led to the downfall of kings much like the revelations and outcry on the internet have forced resignations of the powerful today. The printed word fueled the Enlightenment Era. We can expect that the networks of today and tomorrow will have a similar historic effect.

TV was another big step in sharing thoughts, ideas, and lifestyles across cultures. Here's the experience of a Chinese American, the only child of six in his family not born in China: "My mom taught me a lot, but whatever influence she had could not compete with what came out of that box [TV]. Popular culture did not reflect the realities of my family, but it was so overwhelming that I became what I saw."[40] Today, the printed word and TV are now joined by streaming media and the worldwide web. Together, they pack a powerful cultural punch.

The world is getting smaller and the net effect stronger and faster. There are almost as many mobile phone subscriptions as there are people

---

[39] "How do Asians celebrate Christmas?" Pulse of Asia,
https://www.1stopasia.com/blog/how-do-asians-celebrate-christmas/
[40] Huie, Wing Young, *Chinese-ness*, 2018

in the world. There are over 280 billion emails sent each day. That's about 36 per person.[41]

In his book, *Guns, Germs, and Steel,* Jared Diamond theorizes that the development of countries through time was strongly influenced by the geographic advantages.[42] Today, in the case of culture, it is the availability of information through electronic means that is becoming overwhelmingly influential. People use the net to seek their place in the world.

In summary, modern communication networks have created a new-to-the-world environment where the very personal thoughts and opinions of others are readily available for consumption. This net effect has a way of altering cultures in a way that has never existed before. It surpasses the printing revolution because it allows almost everyone to publish content and make it instantly available and effortlessly searched. I'd like you to consider an important, related question. Does the process of homogenizing cultures through the increased sharing of information produce a new culture or does it simply kill the cultures it homogenizes?

Answers to the Viral Quiz

Remember the ton of watermelon that was thrown in the massive food fight? In a country where many of the older residents have experienced extreme hunger, the idea of throwing food is probably not going to be welcomed. The answer is b: The event was considered wasteful. People asked who took responsibility for cleaning it up. Perhaps there were some cultural messages being transmitted:

- Food is not to be wasted.
- Stress does not relieve one of responsibility.

Now for the two high-achieving university students who were dating. The answer is d: Both students were held up as successful examples of balancing schoolwork and romance. A heart-warming response.

---

[41] Palgrave Macmillan (Ed.). (2020). *The Statesman's Yearbook 2020: The Politics, Cultures and Economies of the World*

[42] Diamond, Jared. (1997). *Guns, Germs, and Steel: The Fates of Human Societies*

Chapter 5

People want to make Sense of the World - Chinese Voices

Chinese Voices - Interview #1

In this China interview, you'll receive the insight of a digital technical manager with exposure to many outside cultures. She takes what I would call a pragmatic approach to managing differences. Would you agree with her assessment of Japanese, Indian, and Latin America tendencies?

Name: 颖怡 (YīngYí "Winnie")

Self-description: Professional, member of a big family, sister
(Born in and lives in China)

I spend a lot of time with my family. I have my husband and a 12-year-old daughter, a younger sister and an older brother. I also have a big family living in the south of China. Those are the most important things in my life.

Cultural Interaction
My job has given me an opportunity to work with people from other countries. When you better understand the working style, then you can work with them well. Europe, Middle East, Latin America, other countries in APAC, they are very different — you need to look at their culture, to find the most effective way.

How to get to know them and their culture? Not easy because one thing is that I have my style. I always do the things in the same way. That's something that I can't control. Need to pay attention, understand their style. There are resources to study, like Globe Smart. Watching a TV or listen to a CD, that is an easy way to learn the cultures.

In the last 20, 30 years, China has changed a lot. From my parents to my generation, to my daughter's generation.

What I have learned from other countries has changed me a lot. I work with people from many different countries. I always have the pressure of different cultures. Like the Indian people, we do support for them. It's a little bit difficult to deal with them, because of the way they handle the work. Another example is when we work with the Japan team. They are polite, but they are not very straightforward. The people from Latin America seem to be very happy.

Digital Influence
I had not talked with my junior high and university schoolmates for 15, 20 years until WeChat [social application in China with over 1 billion monthly active users]. *This has been a dramatic change. Even*

my parents, my mom, who graduated many years ago, found some old schoolmates that now live in many places. The information is overwhelming. I spend maybe 50 percent of my time doing email. I am not able to live without my phone. Everything is in the phone. In China, even at dinner, people are still playing with their phone. When I am in the U.S. at a dinner, I try to leave the phone alone because that is the lifestyle there.

Culture in the Future

In the future, the cultures will be more similar, because of the technology which can reach everywhere. If you look at the kids in China, they love the movies stars of Korea, they love the products of India. They can look at the anime from Japan. I think the culture will be more similar, but not the same. The physical place you are living is still important.

Chinese Voices - Interview #2

Here's a different perspective from someone who grew up in China but has lived in the U.S. and raised a family there. As a Chinese immigrant, she shares her personal challenges and instructs us on cultural nuances to navigate. At this point in her life, do you see her as a Chinese American or an American Chinese?

Name: 瑞玲 (Ruìlíng)
Self-Description: Mother of three; housewife wannabe
(Born in China, living in U.S.)

Cultural Barriers

I was born in north China. After I graduated from college in China, I moved to the U.S. In moving to the U.S., the most challenging part is not the culture shock, not the economic differences, but the language. I can read and write English, but I can't understand people talking. When you study a foreign language, that takes extra effort. My expectation for a job was probably lower than if I would have stayed in China.

Here, actually, if you look around, there are lots of opportunity. Maybe for my situation, I feel a disadvantage because of the language barriers — a psychological barrier, perhaps. If I am where I grew up, there would be more confidence. People look at me. First, I am Asian, and I am a woman, and my English wasn't that perfect. People don't give me the full credit. People that I work with for a long time, they have very great feedback for me, but if I just meet people at the beginning, they don't think I may have the technical background to do what they need to have done. Have a stereotype. I need to work harder than others to prove myself.

The big difference between the U.S. and Asia is the way people deal with conflicts. In China, if you have conflicts, you don't confront them. You try to avoid. You may not discuss but if you discuss, you do it a little bit differently. But here, my guess is that people probably want to bring the issues onto the table to discuss openly.

In China, at least for my generation, you are expected to do good things and expected to be rewarded. It's not like I need to go ask the boss and say I did great things, and you need to reward me. But here, you have to promote yourself to others. If you are silent and do things, no people will see it.

Culture in the Future

In future years, what is to become the day-to-day life? People talk about self-driving cars, natural language translation with your phone so you don't have to learn 10 different languages to go everywhere. Travel may become much easier, and people may see different cultures, they don't see shocks anymore.

I still remember, first several months that I came here and lived in the neighborhood. I was probably the only Asian there and the kids, maybe 4, 5 years-old, they never see people like me. They stare at me. So probably that's to become the norm [to experience other nationalities more often]. *I think another way, the economic differences, is the gap going to be bigger or going to be smaller? When I was in China, it was socialist and moving to communist. Everyone should be equal. The professor and the janitor, they make the same, there is no difference. Right now in China, you see the gap is much bigger.*

I think there will still be differences. My belief is that it is hard to persuade people to change their beliefs. I came from China, I go to church and they try to persuade me to believe in God. I am still questioning it. It's not that I am thinking which one is more believable and which is not, it's just hard for me to believe in one thing when so many different religions exist. My idea is that parents will continue that way, to educate their kids to make sure that is the only one they believe, so that it is passed on to generations.

I think there is much difference in the next generation in China. The next generation, younger than me, the single-child policy makes the kids, I think, more selfish, less responsible, more money-driven. When we grow up, I won't say is a good thing, but the common socialism, it still gives some expectations to people. I won't say the socialist is correct, but you do your work, expectations to meet certain moral standards, they are there.

My Observations and Reflections

In contrast to Eseniia's evolving approach, Winnie discloses that she has her own style. She always does things in the same way. To elevate the productivity of her interactions in other countries, she uses available resources to better understand the general working style rather than modifying her own style. Still, she highlights many changes in China through the generations and in herself from her global interactions. I'd like you to think about Eseniia and Winnie as I describe the Liquified Life in an upcoming chapter. Are they both exercising the liquid flexibility that this theory promotes? Without it, would they be frustrated and ineffective?

Ruiling, having lived in the U.S. for years, has come up with her categorization of Chinese and American behavior, especially in the workplace. To a degree, she is comparing her experience in the U.S. to the China of her youth. In fact, she acknowledges the cultural changes in China when she describes the next generation. This new digitally connected generation is shifting from shared socialistic ideals to a life that expects the world to meet its individual demands. If it takes a village to raise a child, will the village care for those that don't share its values? Now, more than ever, each of us must find a balance between the ideals of past cultures and the many directions now available.

The theme running through these two interviews is a desire to **make sense of the world**. Both are exposed to worlds outside of their upbringing. Both must manage other cultures to succeed. Winnie does research to understand other cultures, cultures in which she must communicate, understand and negotiate. Out of necessity, she categorizes people and makes some general observations. I call this categorization her cultural mind-map, something that will be covered further in a later chapter.

Ruiling is surrounded by the predominate American culture. To survive, she observes the differences between her socialist upbringing in China and her current environment. As an employee, she's learned some of the unspoken means to get ahead. As a mother, she paves the way for the success of her children. As an Asian American, she's concerned about the changes she is seeing in modern China. No doubt, her kids have relied on her to interpret the complexities of life as an Asian American, to make sense of the world for them. No doubt, her kids have mirrored back to her the gaps between her thinking and the American culture they've begun to embrace.

Most of us are experiencing interaction with people outside of our native culture in our work and home environments. We try to make sense of this expanded world, seeking to understand behaviors and beliefs that seem odd or confusing. There are language barriers. Our interaction is often fleeting. Yet for those like Winnie and Ruiling whose work requires productive interaction with a diverse population, seeing the world through different eyes can be rewarding, even life changing.

The neighborhood center where I am a tutor has been around for 20 years or so. When I volunteered for the center, I was told that the kids were from immigrant families. Given the location of the center, I figured that the kids would be Hmong. I had worked with Hmong kids in one of the nearby high schools. On my arrival at the center for my first day of tutoring, I was surprised to see Black kids. Over the year, as I worked with these kids, my cultural mind-map was continually being adjusted. Most of these kids are from Ethiopian immigrant families and are primarily Muslim. As I worked with the kids, I was filling in the significant holes in my cultural understanding.

After failing to give much help to the high school kids on advanced algebra and statistics, I requested the 6th grade as my responsibility. It was a good fit. Even though most evenings spent there are chaotic, they are always rewarding. The kids were filling in their mind-maps, too. They have many questions (Why are your eyebrows so hairy?) and are always eager to see pictures of my family and cat on my cell phone. As I learned later, the center has transitioned from its origin as a church-based tutoring center for a Black congregation to Hmong, to Karen (an ethnolinguistic group of Sino-Tibetan language-speaking people), and to its current population. What a rich history.

I feel extremely blessed by my time there, and I wish everyone could have a similar experience. We are living in an increasingly diverse world, inundated with information. The opportunities for meaningful face-to-face interaction with people outside our inner circle are so precious.

Cultural Mind-Map

We expect meaning in the patterns we see because, in a random universe, it takes energy to create order. (Satell, 2015)

My biggest shock living [in the U.S.], and it bothers my kids as well, is to fill out a form and specify your ethnicity. In Sweden, you never ever tick a box about your ethnicity. (Swedish voice, Lars)

"It's hip to be square." (Huey Lewis and the News, 1986)

I'm going to assume that you are a curious person. After all, you've read this far in this exploration of the new multicultural world. This curiosity aligns well with our first two cultural essentials, "Finding your place in the world" and "Making sense of the world." They are information-intensive activities.

Culture is an adopted pattern of actions and ideas. There are an infinite number of patterns, but people tend to gravitate to recognizable patterns that are shared by others. In other words, most people feel more comfortable as a member of a familiar group. Why? It seems to be in our nature.

Most human characteristics relate to increasing chances of survival and procreation. Having the backing and support of a group has historically been a practical advantage and is central to the existence of cultures. Knowing that, it's fascinating to understand what groups an individual belongs to.

Think of any social situation and you'll see groupings of people: high school, college, work. Think back to high school. Did you strongly identify with a group? Were you labeled? Can you recall the various categories of students that everyone seemed to know? One could call this classification a high-school taxonomy. The names for the groupings often change although the "nerd" label has survived multiple generations. No matter how smart, strong, or beautiful, all humans need a high school survival strategy.

Group dynamics are fascinating and complex. No wonder the "Survivor" reality show has lasted so many seasons. There, in a manufactured environment with intentionally constructed groupings and set rules, people influence, deceive, realign, and attack, all to survive and win. Group or team victories have practical value, even though the competition comes down to an individual.

In a science fiction story, authors begin with a wide-open blank slate, bound only by their own imagination. Yet the stories they create are often filled with different competing groups, frequently with wildly different physical and mental characteristics. It's evidence that group and group behavior are key components of human and non-human experience. It's worth noting that people also seem fixated on those individuals that are uniquely created and set apart. Consider the Marvel universe of characters. Would it be a stretch to say that for many humans a group membership is OK, but that the ultimate desire is to be an independent, one-of-a-kind creature?

That group affinity of ours is a tendency that promotes the bonding of cultures. Of course, as you might suspect, the dynamics of today's society put a whole new spin on this grouping tendency.

Here's a controversial topic of its own. Membership in a group has all sorts of implications. You might disagree, but membership generally will get you preferential treatment. That sounds ideal, when it means one person in a group is willing to help another in the group when in need.

The negative side is when preferential treatment spills into decisions that would normally be for the good of all.

Hold on. I might step on a few toes here. What I suggest is a dichotomy: two mutually exclusive, contradictory ideals regarding groups. The one ideal is that people recognize and belong to groups, that membership and loyalty to a group is admirable, and that reciprocal supporting behavior within a group is a positive force. The other ideal is that people should demonstrate equality and fairness by turning off those group loyalties in many situations. In other words, love the group, but don't let it affect your decisions. Possible?

Group loyalty is an honored part of human nature, yet we see an expectation that people be able to undo these strong feelings and tendencies at the drop of a hat. It's like people are unwilling to recognize that they aren't always in control. Furthermore, people tend to identify with multiple groups that can overlap, converge, and disagree.

Context switching is complicated: "One minute I'm a woman, then I'm an employee of Walmart, then a Texan, then an American, then a human being." Even the membership criteria and the expectations for members are not clear. Does being a woman mean that you must love chocolate? Put that together with the fact that even basic groups are not clearly defined in today's world. For example:

- Woman or man – is it determined by the chromosomes or how someone identifies?
- Employee of Walmart – Full time employee, part-time employee, or contract worker?
- Texan – Live in Texas, born in Texas, pay taxes in Texas?
- American – Think about it. People in Chile are Americans, too. South Americans.

In other words, the world has become a very complicated place, where living up to our own expectations is challenging. Always doing the right thing at the right time for the right group can be beyond reach, as well as beyond definition.

Speaking of groups, let me start out by asking you, dear reader, how you would describe yourself. Just fill in the blank here: I'm _____ . If you can, do it three times with a different answer. Easy? Hard?" As you read the voices from various countries, you can see their answers to this question.

I will bet that for one or more of these answers, you used a family relationship. I'm a mother/father, son/daughter, wife/husband, or something similar. Another one might be an occupation such as teacher, doctor, salesperson, etc. My guess is that you didn't say, "I'm a Caucasian" or "I'm an Asian" or "I'm an African American." Most people, based on my experience, don't identify themselves in that way even though it is perfectly legitimate. Also, very few identify with a country. Yet in many situations, using race and country of origin is how people think of others.

Categorization serves a very important purpose for humans in addition to grouping. In the big picture, what's the most important objective for a species? I think that it's self-preservation, in other words, staying alive and producing a new generation.

What we have seen is that people have a drive to "fill in the blanks." What do I mean by that? Whenever a person meets someone, or sees a picture, or reads about someone unfamiliar, they have a strong tendency to fill in the information they don't know. As noted above, there are all sorts of ways this is done.

Let's say that you're in a new place, and you see someone interesting, someone you'd like to meet. Immediately, humans start gathering data and making assumptions. Based on what can be seen or heard — accent, clothes, hair style, skin condition, observed interactions — humans will form a theory and come to conclusions. Do I take a chance and talk to him or her? Here are four areas of categorization:

- By association: who does this person hang out with?
- By appearance: what does this person wear, what style hair, what body shape?
- By behavior: what has this person done?
- By category: age, gender, race.

As far as we can tell, everyone does this. Would you agree? Fundamentally, people determine whether another person is a threat or an opportunity. They use their memory and processing power, which is quite amazing in its own way, to figure out how to approach the unknown.

OK. Hold on. I'm about to get quite blunt again. Here it is. Humans, even with all our experiences, memory, and processing power, are typically wrong in categorizing new contacts, quite wrong. I am not the only one to believe this. Malcolm Gladwell in *Talking to Strangers* investigates how people assess others they don't know, often in error and with misplaced confidence.

Let's give it a try. Take a look at the picture. I am intentionally not giving you any clues. What do you think? Any ideas where this person is from? How old? Occupation? Where is she going?

I bet you had some initial thoughts. You can't help it. And to be honest, how likely is it that you're correct? We are very, very good at assembling the data we have, it's just that our data is often skewed, and human emotions get in the way. Fortunately, we are also very good at revising categorizations given new data, when we keep our minds open.

I've heard that the human visual system is the most advanced pattern recognition system in the world. Humans see a collection of colors and lines and pull it all together in a flash. Which is why pictures are used online to distinguish real humans from computers. Scientists still don't understand how people can do such fast and refined facial recognition. You see someone after 10 years and he has grown a beard, and you still recognize him in a few milliseconds.

Here is another categorization puzzle. Do you ever eat candy that comes in a variety of colors? I'm sure that you've seen products like this. It's not by accident. With candy, people see value in variety. Through experience and marketing, your mind has been taught to associate colors with flavors. When you eat a yellow one, you are likely to think it tastes different than a red one. But I'm not so sure that's the case. Try a blind taste test sometime.

People like to name things, wouldn't you agree? It seems that once people start using a name for a collection of people, they are reluctant to alter their perception. There is a danger in that tendency, as it can lead to stereotypes, prejudice, and racism. It's best if we think of people as individuals, not a category. Because of my broad experience with people from other countries, I was often asked to present on international topics. For these sessions, I took a variety of approaches, including group exercises and arranging presentations from my global colleagues. Care was required to balance the characterization of a culture with reality. Following a series of meetings on international topics, I traveled to Japan with members of my U.S. team. On a walk back to the office, one U.S. co-worker asked me, "Am I acting appropriately with our Japanese team?" I got the sense that he wanted a pat on the back, and I gave him one. But I was also uncomfortable. The true answer needs to come from the individuals on the Japanese team, not me. And it's not a simple yes or no.

There's a point that I want to make about human capability. Humans are just beginning to learn about how their brains work, neuroscience. So many of our thoughts and feelings are driven by processing that is out of our control. Yet humans are expected to turn off incredible built-in functionality and replace it with an emotionally satisfying cultural framework with all its rules. That's not easy.

Sorry, I'm getting distracted. Let me recap my assertions:

- Humans generally like to belong in groups, which is a foundational element of cultures. These groups influence how people treat each other.

63

- Humans are categorizing stuff all the time using their experience, knowledge, inference, visual pattern recognition, etc. It is what they do, for various reasons that seem to be important.
- While human capacity for categorization is amazing, conclusions are often wrong. Think hidden bias.

For ease of reference, let's call this categorization scheme a cultural mind-map. It's a map of people that people build in their mind through input and filters. People get assigned to categories and categories are arranged in group relationships and hierarchies. This categorization happens in people, whether they want to or not. It's used to navigate through the sea of people in life, much like a geographical map gives directions to driving. This behavior helps us satisfy the cultural need for making sense of the world.

Are you familiar with mind-maps and relationship diagrams? In the case of mind-maps, categories are broken down into branches, much like a tree. In the case of relationship diagrams, names of things go inside boxes. Arrows, symbols, and descriptions in diamonds illustrate the relationships between things. These diagrams can represent how you categorize concepts in your mind.

Let's put the categorization concept of a cultural mind-map together with other concepts we've discussed.

- **Net Effect** – The ability of online interaction to build and alter cultures in ways that have never existed before.
- **Cultural Mind-map** – The tendency for humans to conceptualize groups and to use these groups to make sense of themselves and others, despite many contradictions and incorrect assumptions.

I am excited to share with you another framework that we all use to make sense of the world, language.

Language

In China, our family name is first, the big thing first. Last name, first name. Family is first. Need to think how what you do will affect your family, other people. (Chinese voice)

My English is so good when I am in the US. I start to think in English. It changes the logic of my mind. How you think is really very different. When I think in English and when I think in Russian, I think differently. (Russian voice, Есения)

I understand how culture can be lost. Some families emphasized English rather than Lao language, but many realized that they were losing something. (Laotian voice, Keo)

Language reflects, molds, reinforces and isolates a way of life. I have found that when we study languages, we better understand human nature.

People within a culture create a language and mold it over time. Children learn their primary language as part of their cultural assimilation. Languages both define people and separate people. For me, nothing is more rewarding than the study and application of language. It's a bottomless pot of learning. Etymology is like digging up an archeological site, discovering when and how a word came into being and usage. Words are not stagnant; their definition and usage changes over time. They reflect the need for a culture to express itself. A sociolect, a social dialect, is a language variation used by a particular social group.

In contrast to many other aspects of our human existence, the use of words is not controlled by a bureaucracy. It's the ability of a word to meaningfully express a relevant concept that brings it to life. In the case of a new or modified word, dictionaries only document what groups of people have already decided.

Given all of this, it's reasonable to claim that a culture has a close relationship to its language and that the culture relies on this language to define itself and the environment it lives in. In my research, there is no better language to illustrate the close relationship of a language to a way of life than Korean. For many people in Korea, their language is a source of nationalistic pride. Its alphabet was developed in the 15th century under the order of King Sejong the Great due to the low literacy rate of the people.

The characters (ㄱ, for example) are nestled neatly together into syllable blocks with other characters. So, the word, 안녕하세요 (good morning), has five syllable blocks and consists of 12 characters. The first syllable has three characters, ㅇ, ㅏ, and ㄴ.

The Korean characters are phonetic. With a limited knowledge of Korean, you can piece together the pronunciation of the popular greeting of 안녕하세요 as "an-nyong-ha-se-yo" simply from reading the characters.

It is a very elegant, although challenging language. To further complicate matters for speakers of English and many other languages, verbs go at the end of the sentence (Baby Yoda take note). For the simple declarative sentence, "Now I am going to the city center," here are the words.

지금 시내에 가요.
Written out in Roman characters, it is "Chigŭm shinae-e kayo."

In a few ways, it is very typical of a Korean sentence. We can break it down.

Korean characters	Pronunciation	Meaning
지금	Chigŭm	Now
시내	Shinae	city center
에	-e	to (preposition, attaches to nouns)
가	Ka	go (verb stem)
가요	Kayo	go (verb stem plus polite ending -yo)

Literally, "Now city center to go." Please notice:
- The sentence doesn't use the word "I".
- The verb is at the end of the sentence.
- The verb has an ending which designates a polite reference.

What can we learn about Korean culture from the language? The Korean language reflects the hierarchical nature of life there. Based on the level of respect due another person, a verb will change form. When talking to a child, close friend, parent, or an official, the verb will take on a different composition, primarily in a suffix. Therefore, every sentence reinforces this hierarchical nature of the culture and each specific relationship. As a result, the language includes 16 different versions of each verb just for the four different tenses of a declarative sentence. For each verb in the manual *500 Basic Korean Verbs*, there are 52 variations to learn. (Fortunately, there are some consistent patterns to follow.)

The Korean language also reflects the expectation of humility in other ways. For example, the personal pronoun "I" is seldom used. Contrast this practice to English in the U.S. where "I" seems to be ever present in dialog.

Here's another example. It is common in Korea to refer to one's wife as 집사람 (chipsaram), which translates to "house person." On the other hand, when referring to someone else's wife, the honorific term 부인 puin is used. It is considered impolite to refer to your own wife in an honorific way. Imagine doing this as a common practice in the United States! In Korea, the standard practice is to speak humbly and avoid jealousy in others. In a later chapter, you'll hear why humility is so important there.

I'd like to cover one more interesting example of an elegant language that is quite different from English, Chinese. With Mandarin Chinese, for each word, one needs to learn:

- How to draw the character(s). Consider that for the 3,000 or so most frequently used characters, there is an average of more than nine strokes per character.[43] Most words have one or two characters.
- The associated sounds. There are 21 different initial consonants, six simple finals, and about 30 compound finals.
- The tone to use for each character (out of the five available).

Getting the sound and tone right isn't easy for a beginner, and it is critical to getting your message across. Pronouncing a syllable with a different tone leads to a completely different word. The word love, 爱, is written in pinyin as "ai." It uses the fourth tone, represented as ài. If one were to pronounce the word with the first tone, āi, it would become 哀, meaning to mourn. With the second tone, ái, it becomes the word 癌, cancer.

The very strong cultural focus on the family in China is woven tightly into Mandarin Chinese. The complexity and detail of the family naming conventions accounts for the person's birth sequence, generation, gender, and unique relationship to the speaker. For example, the oldest son is the 哥哥 (gēge) and the oldest daughter is the 姐姐 (jiějie). The younger son

---

[43] Tsai, Chih-Hao. (1996). Frequency and Stroke Counts of Chinese Characters. Chih-Hao Tsai Technology Page, http://technology.chtsai.org/charfreq/

is the 弟弟 (dìdi) and the younger daughter is the 妹妹 (mèimei). You get the idea. It seems that every person has a unique identifier. You can impress your friends by knowing the Chinese name for your father's brother's daughter who is younger than yourself (堂妹 – tángmèi). Another Chinese cultural practice is noted in a quote at the start of this chapter; when referencing the full name of a person in Chinese, the family name comes first, before the given name. Family is prioritized before the individual.

Having touched on Korean and Chinese, it's a good time to introduce the concept of Linguistic Relativity. This is the notion that languages shape the way people see the world and the way they interact with it. This argument has been around in academia for years. Linguistic relativity is based on two assumptions. The first is that a person's language affects his thought. The second is that differences between languages lead to differences in the way people think. (Our Russian friend agrees. Note the relevant quote at the start of this chapter.)

Through these examples, I hope you can see how language reflects the values of a culture. As the language is learned, the perspective of the language molds thought. As a language is used, the structure, rules and usage reinforce cultural ideals. Furthermore, for a human to learn a language, he must embrace it. By embracing it, they can't help but be influenced by it.

While a language can reflect and represent a culture, it is also a barrier to your shared cultural understanding. While a picture is worth a thousand words, most situations require words to communicate our ideas and thoughts. Although it is a considerate gesture to learn a few words to exchange greetings and best wishes in a foreign language, people are barely breaking the surface with such exchanges. The complexity of achieving true fluency points out how much is imbedded into a language beyond the set rules. Translation tools are limited. Language is a big factor in cultural misunderstandings. Often, in immigrant families, kids aren't much interested in learning their parents' language in great depth, just enough to get by. This choice of language can be a proxy for choice of a culture.

English tends to be the language of business. Worldwide, there are over a billion non-native speakers of English, compared to 375 million or so native speakers. That's over twice as many non-native speakers of

English than native ones! This is no accident. Many countries are offering English instruction earlier and earlier in the school curriculum. Many parents see English comprehension as a competitive advantage for their children. That's good news for a shared understanding of culture, but also a reflection of how the Western world is creeping into other cultures.

Our conclusion, that language and culture are closely entwined, could mean a similar fate for both. Languages are not immune to the changes that cultures are experiencing. UNESCO (United Nations Educational, Scientific, and Cultural Organization) predicts that without intervention, half of the over 6,000+ languages spoken today will disappear by the end of this century. It's happening at a rate of about one every two weeks. UNESCO also speaks of the cultural heritage that is embedded in languages.[44]

Furthermore, UNESCO claims there is a link between language and traditional knowledge regarding biodiversity. Many local and indigenous communities have lived for generations in the same natural environment and have developed complex classification systems for the natural world that supports their way of life. Is it any surprise that as the natural world starts to suffer under the weight of human development, these cultures might lose the language that uniquely defines their relationship to the environment?

Cultures clearly benefit from a rich and familiar language intimately connected to personal experiences and native environments. There are two major threats to this comfortable symbiosis. One is the disappearance of culturally bound native language as other languages gain prominence or relevance. The other is the significant challenge to learn another language for acceptance by a new culture. As many around the world have experienced, a transitional state is often uncomfortable and isolating. One is no longer accepted by the old, and not welcome in the new. Fortunately, people can be very good at adapting, as you'll see in the following interviews.

---

[44] Moseley, Christopher (Ed.). (2010). Atlas of the World's Languages in Danger. UNESCO Publishing

Chapter 6

People Adapt
Venezuelan & Honduran Voices

Venezuelan Voice

Moving from Cuba to Venezuela to the U.S. could be a traumatic journey. While living in Venezuela, the country went from an open, receptive society to xenophobic chaos. What is it about this person that allowed her to adapt so smoothly?

Name: Sunny

Self-description: Happy mom, happy wife, software engineer (Born in Cuba, moved to Venezuela at age 6, moved to the U.S. at 35.)

Venezuelan Culture

Venezuelan culture is very rich because our country received people from many countries around the world after World War II: Italy, Spain, France, Germany. They fell in love with our country and married someone there. You can feel their influence in the food. Back then it was easy to get into the country, to work there. Venezuela has beautiful beaches on the east and in the south, mountains and forest.

The immigrants embraced the country and culture in a sharing environment. The food, music, and dances reflected a combination of cultures. In my family, my mom integrated Cuban food with the Venezuelan food. My dad used to play the guitar and sing songs from Cuba.

Kidnapped Country

Today, Venezuela is a totally different country. Everything has changed there. With (Hugo) Chavez, we were really having a hard time with the government. After I left, things got much worse. The government was pushing for the foreigners to leave. It is a totally different world now. If we get a new leader that really cares about the country, I would have hope, but it will never go back to how it was. Even before Chavez, we were having problems. The country will require a totally new redesign. I am not feeling optimistic. I am talking to a lot of people, doing reading and research. The country has been kidnapped. It will never be the same. What is happening is very sad and it is going to get worse.

Transition to the U.S.

With my transition to U.S., the first three years were not easy. I needed to get experience before people would take a chance with me to give me a job. I did some freelance work to get more experience. My first full-time job was in the corporate world, so that made things easier. I was in a better position because I knew how to speak English.

After the first years, it was easy for me to integrate to the country. There was already a lot of influence from the U.S. in Venezuela when I lived there. Now I am married and have a 5-year-old boy. I do not feel like an outsider now because I have family here. In the U.S., I changed my eating habits, partially because of deaths in my family due to cancer. Now I am vegetarian.

Right now, I think of myself as an American.

Digital Influence

Digital makes people a little bit more united. We have social media networks now. I feel closer to people that are far away. I have a sister-in-law in Norway. We used to talk every week.

But digital can separate you from others who are close to you. I used to criticize my daughter because she was glued to the phone. The only way to have a conversation with her was to take the phone away from her for a while.

Cultural Future

I don't think we will be one culture. We will learn more about other cultures and participate a little bit in them. We can use social media and get to know about people's culture. I created a new Instagram account called "My Salads." I search for different foods. When I find a picture of food that I like, I try to contact that person and say, "I like your picture, can you give me your recipe?" Then I try the recipe and I give them some feedback. I am not taking her culture, I am trying out that culture, an exchange. I don't think of people having just one culture. Everybody has many cultures, and they can share their cultures.

Honduran Voice

We just heard from Sunny, a person who chose to leave Venezuela and adapt to a new country. In the following interview, we hear from Yessenia, who is determined to stay and adapt to the demands of her native land, Honduras.

Name: Yessenia
Self-description: Creative, happy, hardworking
(Born and living in Honduras.)

In my country, it's a beautiful place to enjoy nature in an original, unique way. We have different food and flavors, high-quality coffee, and handmade products. People of Honduras are friendly and willing to share cultural experiences.

Digital Influence

Digital has been helping to bring awareness of different places in Honduras to others outside of the country. Digital makes some of the places well known. Helps the economy by encouraging and facilitating tourism. Digital allows people to keep in touch with their families, many of whom are outside of the country. Helps us to be more open-minded, in a very positive way. We get to know other countries and respect their cultures as well. Digital brings people closer to the ones that are farther, farther from the ones that are close.

Cultural Changes

To be honest, there is a kind of change in the culture. Many people in our country are not learning as much about where they live. Here in Honduras, some people try to adopt other lifestyles, losing most of what we did before in our history.

Many of us have been working hard and struggling, not to leave our country, but to make changes to make our country better. The government needs to improve a lot, to provide and enhance our way of life. They need to improve the basic needs, the road conditions. We, the people, are so stressed out about the country. If the government could improve the basics, we could spend more time on improvements to our lives.

My Observations and Reflections

I remember my time in Venezuela. I arrived shortly before an election and Chavez political posters were everywhere. On our late drive from the airport to my hotel, I was asked to look at the lights dotting the hillside above us. "It's beautiful," I exclaimed. "Yes," my host agreed, "but what looks like a glamorous city is a hillside of poverty. You'll see in the morning." My initiation to the world of Venezuela had begun.

Sunny's life was profoundly impacted by her transitions. She emigrated from Cuba to Venezuela to the United States. While many struggle mightily to deal with the cultural implications of migration, Sunny has made it work. Even though many of her formative years were in Venezuela, she is now at peace with considering herself an American. In contrast, my friend Blanca from El Salvador has been in the U.S. for almost 20 years and knows very little English. She spends most of her time raising her four kids. She will do anything to advance their future.

With her Cuban, Venezuelan, and American experiences, Sunny could be considered multicultural. It's a label that many in the world could use. I see it as a positive attribute. Think of the many people and rich influences that Sunny has encountered. Yet multiculturalism is a key element of the situation the world is facing. Because of the factors that were covered in the first few chapters, fewer and fewer people are wholeheartedly adopting a single culture. When this happens, a person loses two benefits. They lose the assurance of the sacred whole, a sense of an established and proven pathway for success. Secondly, they are at risk of losing a community of fellow believers.

What they gain, if they can manage, is an adopted culture that better matches their individual experience and beliefs. It's a brave step to take and a necessary one for a person like Sunny, whose complex life can't be constrained to a simple pathway. I have friend from China and a friend from Malaysia who fell in love long distance, married, and are living in Singapore. They are managing the inevitable cultural complexity and are focusing on what they share, a love of family and the importance of education. This book seeks to acknowledge these trends and demonstrate that updated support systems are required for this new way of life.

I volunteer in a non-profit organization, Conversations with Friends (CWF), that seeks to support people in ICE (Immigration and Customs Enforcement) detention in our area. As part of this involvement, we meet regularly with Spanish speaking people who are in ICE detention at one of the local for-profit facilities. It's a heart-breaking and heart-warming experience. It's heart-breaking to see a parent who has lived in the U.S. for over 20 years being separated from his family through deportation, fighting back tears. On the other hand, it is heart-warming to see how people from many different countries come together and support each other through a tremendously trying experience. As I meet new inmates, I often see people who would appear to be hardened criminals in orange jumpsuits, their arms crossed and their expressions grim. As they introduce themselves, I hear gratitude and openness. Each person has his story and makes contributions to the group. We've seen people step up and become facilitators, helping to welcome, accommodate, and support new detainees, regardless of the new person's country of origin and ability to speak Spanish. When motivated, people can adapt and break barriers.

Yessenia lives in a country where emigration to the U.S. is commonplace. Yet she has made the decision to stay in her country of birth. She is currently in a program supported by Honduras and the U.S. to teach Honduran small business owners best practices for growing their enterprises. She spent six weeks in the U.S. learning how to better manage the soil and water use on her family's small farm.

People are driven to make their lives better. As cultural guidelines become inconsistent or irrelevant, some people are willing to move on to what works. If cultural guidelines are a master plan to ensure economic and social success, deviation from those guidelines introduces risk. But what we are seeing in much of the world today is that people are willing to take that risk and find their own individual formulas. They are willing and able to adapt.

Just ahead of the global pandemic, I traveled through Honduras. What is the real Honduras? My Honduran friends and I toured the ruins of the advanced Mayan culture with a local guide and later made small talk with a machine-gun-toting soldier at a checkpoint. We watched a traditional small-town parade that included a giant Peppa Pig, a popular character from a British preschool animated series. While at a bustling coffee shop, I experienced kindness and closeness that I associate with Latinx families.

I am convinced that the world needs to support a new equilibrium of shared culture and individual pathways. Will this happen naturally, or are we better off being proactive? I believe the solution will come easier if we first recognize the gap.

How about you? Are you content with your current cultural framework and your relationships with others outside that framework?

The Liquified Life

With global access, people will be more and more connected. We are going to get lost under a pile of data. Maybe you will see a culture of people online. Arts will go on and everything will be accepted. Maybe different types of expression will come, an online halo experience. (Iranian voice, ساقی)

I have arrived at a concept that I call the "Liquified Life." Let me explain. Many years ago, life was a great deal more isolated, more stagnant. By stagnant, I mean that within a lifetime, people matured, and their world changed at a slower pace. From one generation to the next, conditions and the environment were relatively stable, at least during peacetime. By stable, I don't mean safe or easy. Families generally lived in the same area and faced similar issues from year to year. People were isolated from other parts of the world, with limited communication. Even as late as 1800, around 97 percent of the world lived in rural areas. Given that distribution, it's likely people did not encounter much diversity. In general, the farther you go back in time, the more this is true, because people lacked the means to change their lives and connect with others outside of their immediate circle.

To me, this concept of "stagnancy" can be represented by solid matter. Once a solid is formed, the size and shape stays the same, unless significant force is exerted. Think of a clay object that's been fired hard inside a kiln. Let's consider many people of the past to be of this solid form. From one generation to the next, one solid person produced another, with not a lot of difference between them. Kids grew up and learned an occupation and a lifestyle from their parents. The household "kiln" established their composition. There wasn't much opportunity to learn about other parts of the world or other cultures. Even traveling to the next city was an effort.

An example from history will help me make my point. In 921 CE, Ibn Fadlan left Baghdad on a dangerous mission to seal an alliance between the Bulgers and the caliph who sent him. It involved a trip of thousands of miles in a large caravan with hundreds of camels. He left the comfortable surroundings of an Islamic world. He and his caravan experienced people who had not adopted Islam and had learned to survive in radically different environments. When these distant leaders were confronted with Ibn Fadlan and the culture he represented, they faced a decision. With the fate of the visitors completely in their hands, how would they respond? Would they exchange them as slaves, annihilate them, or peacefully exchange gifts? On the journey at the camp of Etrek, the foreign nobles debated Idn Fadlan's fate for days. In the end, Ibn was permitted to leave in peace, and he rewarded his hosts with lavish gifts.[45]

Ibn Fadlan was a courageous traveler who experienced many hardships and radically different cultures. Over the course of his journeys, he seemed to possess an uncanny ability to face these cultural encounters and escape with his life (no doubt with bribes and clever negotiations). The fact that he even interacted with other cultures was very unusual for his time. He carefully documented his observations of the environment and foreign customs in his memoirs.

Now consider the effort that Fadlan and his fellow travelers expended just to meet their neighbors. They traveled long distances over hostile territory with a large caravan that was only possible due to the support of the wealthy caliph. As they met other cultures along the way, they risked their lives. In the end, their mission was unsuccessful. Once Almish, the

---

[45] Gordon, Stewart. (2008). *When Asia was the World*

leader of the Bulgers, realized that Ibn Fadlan did not have the money promised him by the caliph for the building of a fort, he rejected the proposal. The money that was to follow Ibn Fadlan on the journey never arrived. No money, no alliance. Fortunately, Ibn Fadlan's memoirs survived.

Is it any surprise that most of the people of that time stayed within their protected environment, having little exposure to any other culture? Interacting with other cultures was difficult, expensive and risky! Generation after generation lived that way. Isolated as they were, their separate cultures were passed down and strengthened with each generation.

Today, the digital nature of our lives dramatically increases opportunities for diverse cultural and personal interaction. Now you've got more data than you know what to do with. From a toddler to a grandparent, the world is there to explore and understand. IBM has estimated that each day 2.5 quintillion of bytes of data are created[46] — that's 2,500,000,000,000,000,000 bytes.

Today, with all this information available about other parts of the world and other ways to live, some people can be much more fluid, adaptable. You've seen that happen. There are people who immerse themselves in the experience and knowledge of others. The constant information flow that they absorb alters their ideas and perceptions. That's what I call the Liquified Life. Their life operates like a liquid, changing shape based on new information received. While solids reject or deflect other objects, liquids absorb them. Turino (2004) recognizes fluidity when he compares "the earlier, homogeneous views of identity, and more recent ideas about identities being fluid, constructed, and multiple."[47]

On the other hand, I realize that even in today's digital world, there are many people who remain fixed, unchanging, and solid. They ignore information altogether or restrict themselves to content and data that reinforces their current position. The tremendous amount of available data gets filtered to what is considered relevant. They surround

---

[46] IBM Research.
https://researcher.watson.ibm.com/researcher/view_group.php?id=4933
[47] Turino, Thomas. (2004). *Identity and the Arts in Diaspora Communities*. p.9

themselves with like-minded Facebook friends, people who share similar ideals. Rather than becoming fluid, people can become stagnant. Perhaps they are overwhelmed?

That information filtering process is enabled by media producers and providers. They use algorithms to determine what content will be read, watched, and liked. They are gathering information about each person's area of interest and history of online choices to determine what to highlight. For example, Netflix knows that if they can continue to surface content that people enjoy watching, these satisfied customers will continue to pay for their service. The problem with all this behind-the-scenes processing is that people are led down a track that reinforces prior decisions rather than broadening their exposure.

While these concerns are real, I think the Liquified Life will be the way of the future. With the knowledge available, the world will become a different and better place for those who pursue it. Knowledge is power. It seems that the proper use of that power requires:

- A free flow of information to discover and share.
- A general consensus on what is real and good.
- The means and motivation to apply knowledge for improvement.

It will take some practice and effort. Everything requires a balance. With most new technologies, it's not the core discovery that leads directly to beneficial change. Rather, it's a long process of iterative adaptation, experimentation, and enhancements.

People are at the stage of discovering the good and bad that results from a transformational change in the availability of information. Take social media. Cyber-bullying is a big thing. Cybercriminals engage in phishing to gain access to personal information. On the other hand, ratings and reviews provide a way for people to share and learn from others' experiences. Shoddy products are exposed, and people have much more information to help them make decisions.

Many of the advances that humans have produced occurred at a time when a strong, stable culture provided a foundation for learning. Let's take another look at Ibn Fadlan. At the time he made his trip, his home of Baghdad was the epicenter of the Islamic Golden Age, an important commercial, cultural, and intellectual center. The people rebuilt canals and dikes, drained swamps, and reduced the impact of malaria. The reigning caliph oversaw great cultural expansion and founded the Academy of Wisdom with a library and an observatory. The study of mathematics, medicine and philosophy flourished, along with the introduction of algebra.

Without this strong culture and stability, I doubt these improvements would have been possible. The sharing of information within the larger Muslim world promoted advancements. In the years ahead, we'll see more and more shared information across the globe, which has the power to transform people. It will take time, but as masses of people reach new levels of understanding, they will learn to deal with the changes to culture and find better ways to live.

There's more we can learn from the story of Baghdad. The Golden Age of Muslim was soon to expire, courtesy of Genghis Khan and the Mongols. Who was Genghis Khan? He was the son of an outcast family who was left to die. He killed his older half-brother, was enslaved by a rival clan, and later escaped, all while a child. He grew up to change the course of history.

It was 337 years after Ibn Fadlan left Baghdad on his mission that the Mongols of Genghis Khan came and destroyed Baghdad. It was a collision of two incompatible cultures. There was a horrific loss of life with perhaps hundreds of thousands of people massacred. In 25 years, the Mongol army subjugated more lands and people than the Romans did in 400 years.

While they decimated the social systems of the lands they conquered, they also pursued lofty international goals, and desired to establish a global order. They worked to institute free trade, a universal alphabet, and paper currency. There was an effort to create a universal basic education system and to make all children literate. They improved the accuracy of the calendar and produced extensive maps.

Due to the general poverty of Europe at the time, the Mongol kingdom declined to conquer and incorporate the cities of Europe into its empire. It did, however, initiate trade with the Polo family of Venice. In addition, envoys permitted exchanges between the Mongol khans and the popes and kings of Europe.

Europe benefited greatly. The Mongol kingdom produced technology that fueled the European Renaissance. Europe adopted their advances and inventions including printing, firearms, the compass, and the abacus. Europeans traded their tunics and robes for Mongol fabrics, pants and jackets. English scientist and philosopher Roger Bacon gave the Mongol empire credit for succeeding beyond the battlefield by learning and applying the principles of philosophy. Jack Weatherford in *Genghis Khan and the Making of the Modern World* went so far as to say that "seemingly every aspect of European life — technology, warfare, clothing, commerce, food, art, literature, and music — changed during the Renaissance as a result of the Mongol influence."[48]

Why do I reach back into history? To learn the lessons of the past and to anticipate the future. We've just mentioned two waves of forced cultural transitions. They took isolated people and made them part of a larger movement. My point is that human history shows us the possibility of great advances as people are brought together in an environment that seeks and uses knowledge to improve life. That's what the Liquified Life will allow.

What are the barriers to this progress? To start with, the world is far from egalitarian. Not everyone has the same access to technology and information. And for those who do have access, the steady bombardment of opinions, rage, and hurtful comments can be overwhelming. The "net effect" of this environment ushers in new extremes. Those conditions can push people over the edge. Suicides are the major cause of death for young adults, and there's a big rise in the rate for young females, who spend much of their life online.

These problems are being recognized. Programs have been initiated to bring better connectivity to rural areas. There is increased sensitivity to the negative effects of doom scrolling.

I am not so naive as to think the Liquified Life will ensure perfect equality. But as they say, a rising tide lifts all boats. Many people will have the opportunity to live the Liquified Life, and benefit from a steady flow of information. Lives and relationships will improve, and better thinking leads to ideas that will help with the issues. With Sunny and Yessenia, we can see how adaptability can work. There is a critical decision point when

---

[48] Weatherford, Jack. (2004). *Genghis Khan and the making of the Modern World*

we are faced with challenging information. Do we take it in, process it, and make informed decisions on how to proceed, or do we act with fear and strike out at others? Equipping people with tools to deal with new situations and ambiguity will increase positive outcomes.

Let me end this chapter with a real-life example of how information, openness, and adaptability have made a big difference in the lives of some impoverished and isolated people in rural China. The example comes from the *China Economic Information Service*, an English news publication of the Xinhua News Agency.[49] Here's my summary of the article.

In Liangshan Yi Autonomous Prefecture, Hu Xiufong could barely make ends meet. He lived in a mountainous region where getting agricultural products to the market was challenging. Fortunately, the leaders of Liangshan explored eCommerce as a means of marketing their products. Hu Xiufong was not a young digital entrepreneur. He was 48 and uneducated, but he pushed forward with the idea of opening an online shop. He started out by sharing the link with everyone he met and offering them a few free apples.

He went from 80 WeChat friends the first year to 3,800 friends four years later. He now earns about $57,000 a year with apples harvested on two hectares of land. Hu established a cooperative that enabled more villagers to sell apples online. Annual sales soon topped $1.4 million, contributing to the income of nearly a hundred poor families.

The difference-maker here is shared information and the willingness to use it. Whether it's Liangshan Yi Autonomous Prefecture in the Information Age, Baghdad in the Islamic Golden Age, or Baghdad as part of the Mongol empire, the ability to adapt even in times of dramatic change defines the Liquified Life.

---

[49] Xinhua News Agency. (Jan 3, 2020). Across China: E-commerce a fast track to prosperity for poor mountainous areas. *China Economic Information Service*

Chapter 7

People want Culture to reflect their Values - Iranian Voice

The interview with Saghi was a long and intense one. Her desire to tell the true story of Iran was clear. Gunshots in the street, subversive kisses, and jumping over fire — these are fascinating revelations.

Name: ساقی (Saghi)
Self-description: Iranian woman, immigrant, researcher, "I try to be a good person."

(Born in Tehran and left Iran in 2009 at age 23 for schools in France, then Belgium and the U.S. Now working in the U.S.)

I want to dedicate this interview to Bahareh Karami and Shadi Jamshidi, two of my beloved friends who were killed as they were returning to Canada from their trip to Iran. They were the passengers of Ukraine International Airlines Flight 752 that was shot by a missile from Iran on Jan. 8, 2020.

I was born and lived in Tehran, upper west side, to an upper-class family. My grandpa was in the military during the Shah era. I went to Teheran's Polytechnic University. In 2008, lots of my friends were leaving the country. In 2009, it was the year of election fraud and protest in Iran. When I was in the streets, I saw people being shot and killed, tear gas in my eyes. At that time, at age 23, I moved to France for a master's degree. The first year was very difficult. I moved several times in the next few years, to Belgium and then the U.S.

Many years ago, my mom went to college in the U.S., and learned the value of knowing other countries and languages. My aunt on my mom's side, she was the first to move out of Iran. On my dad's side, I have two uncles and one aunt who moved to Sweden. My mom always had this idea that we had to go. I thought that I would travel and be back. I have to be with my family and support. I have a duty. I felt guilty. Now we have a travel ban, so my parents can't come to the U.S. I have voted in the last Iranian elections, but I am not thinking of going back there to live.

When I was first in the US, I had a single-entry visa — with this visa, if you leave, you need a new visa to return, which is always a risk. On applications for a visa there is a question, "Is your nationality one of these locations? North Korea, Iran ….".

Social Interaction
Iranian communication is subtle. Poetry is subtle. Even our news is subtle. Read the signs, read between the lines, that is something that really does happen. Among the people, there are subtle challenges to

the current government. In Belgium they kiss once, in France twice. In Iran, kisses are three, three kisses all the time — right, left, right — I don't know why, it happened after the revolution. Before the revolution, there was one kiss. Some people will use one kiss to subtly indicate that they are supportive of the former regime, the Shah.

Women will stretch the rules, wearing their scarf loosely, exposing their hair. Cultures that I feel the closest to are those that have experienced the same socialist oppression. Now people will tell me, I don't have time to protest. But some people will say [to the government] that the U.S. is going to invade you, so you better listen to us.

In practice, men and woman do not shake hands in public. You don't see hugging or kissing on TV, it is censored. Of course, when you are alone, you can do whatever. Girl's and boy's schools are separated from first grade to college, and we wear uniforms.

Many Iranians have immigrated, so that kind of core family mentality has changed. You don't grow up in the same city. You come and go. Used to be in my grandma's time that people all lived close together. Currently, families only have one or two kids. Now everyone is so scattered for jobs or education. We used to live in a series of apartments with a garden or pool in the middle. We used to have yards and gardens.

Digital Influence

People are working hard to get information. The state TV is considered as an arm of the government since the Supreme Leader chooses the Head of Islamic Republic of Iran Broadcasting. The internal news media companies are also closely monitored by the judicial branch. When younger, I used Tor (a dark web browser) every day of my life. The dark web was our friend. In Iran, the Internet is censored and is shut down when there are conflicts. On TV, there were only two channels, channel 1 and channel 2. We used Viber to get information. With Viber, we had a group of my family and friends, old and young. It has a purple logo with a phone. Viber got censored, so a lot of people went to Telegram, a Russian company. It gave you the possibility of making your own channel. In general, I see the digital capabilities as an absolutely positive thing. I think we will be becoming more global online. When one is exposed to external sources, they will no longer be satisfied with what was previously forcibly offered by the state.

Some values are changing, because, for example, your mom and dad are not the people who know the most, your uncle or aunty is not the person who knows the most, Google knows the most. We were told, don't say something above what an elder person told you. Who are you to object? That is changing because people have access to facts.

Religious and Cultural Diversity

Iran is a big country with many different people. It's beautiful how people can stand each other. It used to be a big empire, now a small one. Kurds, always a minority, always suppressed, have a rich, rich culture. They have their own language. Very much in touch with nature. People in Iran do feel that they belong to the land and the history. It is the cradle of civilization. Many people will first introduce themselves as Persians which connects them with their history. The Silk Road is something that people are proud of.

My family had a religious background. I was not forced to practice but was sometimes guilted to practice. In Iran there are Muslims, both types. Christians and Jews are a minority. There are differences in the beliefs of Sunni and Shia. In Iran, they have Shia teaching in school, mention Sunni beliefs and why Shia think that Sunni is wrong.

We have ancient Iran Zoroastrian celebrations. On the longest night of the year, I remember how we stayed up all night and ate pistachios. On the New Year, we have seven bonfires, and jump over them. My sadness will go to the fire. Fires are holy, but we don't pray to fire or worship it. Kids go to houses, knock on doors with spoons like trick or treat in the U.S. On April 1, we go outside, celebrate in nature, and tell lies like April Fools in the U.S.

From Zoroastrianism, we are taught to say good things, do good things, think of good deeds. They had corruption, but I think that every cleric has some corruption. We practiced extreme politeness, called Taarof, asking even for simple things, "Can I do that?" Or say "My apologies," if you are sitting with your back to someone. People argue back and forth about who would pay the bill, until someone gives up. I am in that age that I will tell the younger ones that, oh, you are very impolite, but my parents thought the very same of me.

Iranians are quite nostalgic. My parents and grandparents say, "Oh, I am thinking of the good times when everything was great." I don't know when that good time happened.

Cultural History

Iranians are proud that we have never been colonized. Invaded, yes, but not colonized. We have the Islamic influence, which Arabs introduced when they invaded. Arabs invaded and raped women, which was terrible. We were taught these are barbarians who invaded us. But as Iranian people learned Arabic, they could learn from scientific texts. Arabic was the language of science. They became interested in astronomy and geometry. Years later, Genghis Khan and the Mongols invaded, stayed and became interested. Some benefits in science came due to increased communication across the larger empire.

I was 3 years old when the war between Iran and Iraq ended (1988), too young to remember it. I was told that we had three warnings, "white" means things are OK, "yellow" means an attack is coming, and "red" means attack is here. Newspapers were black and red. I remember the first time that I saw a newspaper in color. When you wanted to buy regular groceries, we would have coupons. You had to stand in line. Parents would stand in line for an hour and a half, and we would play.

Culture in the Future

Culture is us, it is not what is imposed on us. What we do, that is our culture. Put a few people together, they will have a culture. We will still have something. I think and I hope that nature will be more celebrated. I look forward to more respect for the trees. With global access, if some countries don't censor, people will be more and more connected. We are going to get lost under a pile of data. Maybe you will see a culture of people online. Arts will go on and everything will be accepted. Maybe different types of expression will come, an online halo experience.

My Observations and Reflections

I agree with Saghi. We will always have culture in one form or another. My concern is that many of our existing traditional cultures seem to be struggling to provide a stable, comprehensive pathway for life. In the case of Iran, a theocratic government is attempting to impose a culture. The primary problem, as I see it, is that people of Iran have ideas, experience, and goals that conflict with the mandated culture. Through increased transparency, the people see the limitations and faults of the cultural path provided to them. They are aware of the options for different values and lifestyles. Furthermore, the turbulent and repressive environment interferes with transferring a truly workable culture from one generation to the next.

For an example, look no further than the protests generated by the killing of Mahsa Amini by the morality police. Iranian women want the freedom to individualize their appearance. Oppression and brutality are being used to enforce a manufactured set of cultural values and to suppress the resulting demonstrations.

From what I have experienced and read, the most sustainable and practical cultural lifestyles are those informed by the experiences, trials and errors of the community within a guardrail of fairness and respect. If we are not able to organically form and sustain a culture, powerful institutions will force one upon us to suit their objectives.

Are you following a cultural pathway that was established by others, say your family or community, religion, or government? Or could your pathway be described more accurately as a patchwork of values that you have personally crafted from all the inputs in your life? If so, have you found a community that shares those values?

Iranian Cultural Transformation

"While these Iranians rejected their own history and imagined a future modeled on the West, Shariati wrote, the common people, welded to local tradition, embraced the past and felt the future didn't belong to them." (*Children of Paradise: The Struggle for the Soul of Iran*, Laura Secor)

"The lies are, above all, a consequence of surviving in an oppressive regime, of being ruled by a government that believes it should be able to interfere in even the most intimate affairs of its citizens." (*City of Lies*, Ramita Navai)

It seems that each country teaches its population primarily about their own history. For many people, learning about other countries in more than a superficial way is a luxury. I suspect that many people around the world do not know much about the interesting history or current internal condition of Iran, beyond the headlines of war, nuclear arms and revolution. I see how it takes a personal connection, your teacher, doctor, neighbor, or co-worker to make a country become real to you. That's one reason I included the "voices" chapters, capturing thoughts of people around the world.

Iran has a long colorful history as one of the earliest civilizations. Its course has been altered by invaders and wars. Currently, it is isolated from the rest of the world. As I write this, the Internet in Iran has been shut down due to ongoing internal conflicts.

In terms of international relations, the U.S. has restricted Iranian visitors, immigrants, and students. U.S. President Donald Trump voided a nuclear arms agreement and reinstituted severe sanctions. On Jan. 3, 2020, the U.S. killed a notorious Iranian general with a drone while he was in Iraq. Days later, Iran retaliated with missile attacks on U.S. troop locations in Iraq. Within hours, a passenger flight from Tehran to Kyiv operated by Ukraine International Airlines was struck down by missiles launched by the IRGC (Islamic Revolutionary Guard Corps). All 176 passengers and crew were killed.

The heightened tensions have put the people of Iran in an even more stressful situation. Those who have dared to protest price increases now fear punishment from the Iranian government at the same time they dread a possible external attack from the U.S. The past and present are carrying Iran through its own dangerous cultural transformation.

Iran has so many examples of our cultural themes, I don't know where to start. The people there are proud of their long history. It's part of their identity. Yet, as in so many other countries, the transformations have accelerated in recent years, and traditional culture is paying a price.

Like Iraq, Iran became primarily Muslim with the invasion of the Arabs over 1000 years ago. Consider the present situation. In just the last 75 years, Iran has had a few defining events that have rocked the government and the social system. If you think that oil was involved, you'd be right. The British-owned Anglo-Iranian Oil Company (now BP) was making a lot of money on Iranian oil. This bonanza was threatened when the oil industry was nationalized by Iran in the early 1950s. That didn't sit well with those enjoying the profits. Prime Minister Mohammad Mosaddegh, who had led the effort toward nationalization, was overthrown in a coup believed to have been orchestrated by British and U.S. intelligence. Mosaddegh was also opposed by religious leaders such as Ayatollah Kashani, who wanted Iran to become an Islamic state. Kashani withdrew his religious support once he could see that Mosaddegh was a firm believer in the separation of church and state.

Not long after that, the Shah returned to power from exile with Western support. He initiated the "White Revolution." There was land reform and modernization. The women's right to vote was won in 1963. But there was also suppression of dissent from the SAVAK secret police. Many people objected to the increased influence of Western values and culture.

Don't make the mistake of thinking that the battle for the hearts of the people and the right to rule was between just two distinct choices, Western vs. Islam. There were many aspiring leaders formulating their plans, making speeches and writing papers. Like any politician, they tested the people's reaction and adjusted accordingly. Some took Western ideas and embedded them into their thinking. They used clever redefining of Islam to position themselves as promoting nationalistic, historic values. Others took elements of Marxism. Some floated the idea that all people could have a direct relationship with God instead of the need for clerics to mediate, a radical concept for Islam.

In some ways, it was a cultural free-for-all. Many people didn't like the shift in values during the Shah's rule. It was not the Iran they knew. (Similar, perhaps, to many people in the U.S. who joined a movement to "make America great again.") In Iran, there were many opposing forces that had very different notions on how to proceed. It was up to the opposition leaders to tap into the shared Iranian experience and present a case for something that could work.

In 1978, the resistance reached a crescendo and the pendulum swung back to more traditional values. The clerics objected to the policies of the Shah, and the people rejected his authoritarian rule and neglect of the poor. Riots ensued. One year later, the Shah was expelled, and the iconic Islamic cleric Ayatollah Ruhollah Khomeini returned from exile. The country became governed as a theocracy with the Ayatollah as the Supreme Leader. The Islamic Republic was born.

Do you remember the American hostages taken by Iran? That happened in the same year, 1979. If that wasn't enough, the Iran-Iraq war started in 1980, and lasted eight years with estimated Iranian casualties of one million people.

In the first 28 months after the start of the new republic in 1979, tribunals reportedly had 757 people executed for corruption. They exhibited no regard for due process. This was more than seven times the number of political prisoners executed than in the final last eight years of the Shah's rule.[50] Still, many welcomed the return to a Muslim focus and saw the ouster of Western influence and money as justified.

After 20+ years of this Islamic Republic rule, what was the mood of the people? I suggest that the awarding of the Nobel Peace prize in 2003 to Shirin Ebadi for her work on human rights was symbolic of the times. Many people were pushed to the limits to follow the rigid religious laws of the state, and resistance was not tolerated. Hence the push for human rights.

The governmental shifts in Iran over the last 75 years have been extreme, but there were some constants. The Shia branch of Islam was consistently the majority religion. The suppression of dissent was another constant, regardless of who was in power. And with suppression comes isolation.

Cultural activities in Iran have become colored by government influence. The mourning for the Assassination of Ali, on the 21st day of Ramadan, is an important holiday commemoration that has political implications. The people of Iran take mourning seriously. Rawda is one of the Shia Iranian public lamentation mourning rituals. In this ritual, a storyteller recites heartrending and somber religious stories and poems. Some people beat their chest with the tempo of the songs. Many families donate free food (Nazri) to the mourners. You might have heard of mourners going to an extreme and using a blade to cut themselves.

Holidays within a country provide insight into widely shared cultural values. Given each country's government involvement in setting and supporting official holidays, there's often a political motivation as well. Changes in holiday observance can track cultural evolution. In the U.S., consider the deemphasis of Columbus Day. For many, the arrival of Christopher Columbus to the Americas is now associated with the initiation of colonization, slave trade, and warfare, not as a historic voyage. Transparency strikes again.

---

[50] Secor, Laura. (2016). *Children of Paradise: The Struggle for the Soul of Iran.* p.35

There is a powerful political and religious significance in the mourning of Ali's assassination, and it represents a core difference between Shia and Sunni Muslims. The Prophet Mohammed personally chose Ali as the Iman and successor. In opposition, Sunni Muslims believe that Muhammed's successor should be chosen by the elders. Iran, with its Shiite majority, can leverage this holiday to reinforce its core values, covering the day's activities on state TV channels.

Many elements were playing out, many of them relevant to our cultural investigation. We have seen how people adjust to shared, oppressive isolation. It's a means of psychological and physical survival. In this extreme environment within Iran, where transparency can cause one potential harm, an honest person is sometimes labeled as stupid or a troublemaker. Top-down culture strictly imposed by the government can be effective in regulating behavior, but it can also generate resentment and workarounds. People are people, after all.

I see technology being leveraged by the powerful to restrict and monitor behavior in the name of security and convenience. The tools are there. In some countries, such as Iran, the interception of email and bugging of phone calls are commonplace. Other countries are implementing more sophisticated tools such as facial recognition. Juniper Research forecasts that 90% of smartphones will have some form of biometric hardware by 2024. Either extreme scenario (the golden age of information or a period of aggressive technology oversight) will lead to the diminishing of traditional culture.

In Iran, despite the strict control, the cat is out of the bag (unlike North Korea, which we'll discuss later). Through the Internet, travel, and education, most people are aware of alternate lifestyles and belief systems, especially among the middle and upper classes that experienced greater freedom before the revolution. There's an uneven, uncomfortable disparity between human reality and the expectations of the state.

Many people are essentially living double lives, one public, another private. Women wear radically different types of clothing when in the streets versus inside the houses of friends and family. To control women's behavior, the state created a morality police force called Guidance Patrol, which has the authority to confront women about their clothing in the streets and bring them to a law enforcement office. At the office, they have their picture taken, pay a penalty, and sign a binding pledge to follow the Hijab dress code. Activists organized the White Wednesday event when women wear white scarfs to signal their opposition to mandatory hijab. Some of these activists were captured and sentenced to multiple years in prison. Amid the protests of 2022, multiple executions were carried out.

In the *City of Lies*, the author highlights experiences of people in Tehran who attempt to navigate the many top-down cultural requirements while addressing their personal needs and goals. Many people have a strong belief in Islam, but they experience a misalignment between their own beliefs and the regulations of the state and clerics.[51]

That's a very difficult environment for a bottoms-up culture. One might hope for a negotiated middle ground with relaxed regulations and increased buy-in. But we've seen how modern generations are now more diverse and individualistic than ever. Surviving as individuals might be preferable to taking on the government. Based on Iran's recent history, a revolution or coup seems more likely than a compromise. Regardless, a revolution would leave much of the population in unfamiliar cultural territory again, ready to listen to a new voice claiming to have all the answers.

Many people have had a taste of mobility and choice, and they won't give it up easily. As part of the modernization of the Shah's rule, the introduction of cinema opened the rest of the world to the Iranian population. However, to many of the demonstrators during the revolution, it symbolized Western corruption. As a result, 195 of Iran's 525 movie houses were demolished.[52] But the destruction of the buildings could not erase the images projected on the screen and etched into the memory of movie-goers.

People crave a structure that helps them make sense of the world, especially in traumatic conditions like this. They want a culture that takes the often-conflicting values in their lives and packages them together in a way that they, their families, and community can adopt, justify, and live with. They want their culture to reflect their values. But for reasons we've discussed, this is becoming increasingly difficult to do in Iran.

---

[51] Navai, Ramita. (2014). *City of Lies: Love, Sex, Death, and the Search for Truth in Tehran*

[52] Secor, Laura. (2016). *Children of Paradise: The Struggle for the Soul of Iran.* p.26

In my opinion, the artificial barriers between what people believe and what they are forced to do will tend to break down around the world. Many governments will manage that transition relatively peacefully, but others will experience the cultural chaos of a revolution. In the absence of a top-down culture, the lack of uniformity and desire for individual self-actualization will mean that a single all-inclusive culture will not fill the void for most people.

I don't see this transition as Western values vs. the world. The individualism that characterizes the U.S. is the natural outcome of the general forces that are affecting cultures. These forces will continue to impact country after country. When people reach the point when no viable wholistic cultures are available in an environment (either organic or enforced), individualism is the last resort. The U.S. has embraced this condition. It has encouraged people to pursue their individual dreams.

There will be a variety of personal reactions to these changes. But as I have already shared through my description of the Liquified Life, those who can navigate through a new, loosely structured society will prevail.

Iran's rocky cultural ride of the last 75 years tells a unique story. Dramatic changes in leadership have seen the cultural pendulum swing back and forth. Even though each new government imposes its own strict rules and obtrusive oversight, the people are aware of alternative lifestyles and the corruption of the ruling class. There is a heightened tension between reality, prescribed behaviors, and each person's aspirations. Yes, people are adaptable, but my theory is that with the increased transparency, instability, and alternatives in the world of today, many people will abandon wholistic traditional culture as a guiding force and seek their own individual path or new forms of culture.

As the recent history of Iran illustrates, people want their culture to reflect their values. How can we represent those values and deal with the inevitable conflict between them? To that end, I'd like to present the concept of cultural vectors.

Vectors and Cultural Contradictions

How can we draw a generalized map of human tendencies relevant to cultures?

I realize that theories and models abound already. Each one takes a different approach to what drives behavior. These models attempt to explain why humans do what they do. Decades ago, Sigmund Freud came up with the concepts of the id, ego and super-ego. In the words of Freud in *The Ego and the Id*, published in 1923, "if the differentiation we have made of the mind into an id, an ego, and a super-ego represents any advance in our knowledge, it ought to enable us to understand more thoroughly the dynamic relations within the mind and to describe them more clearly."[53] Intriguing.

Freud is famous for his work on individual behavior. We are analyzing group behavior. I'd like to share my concept of the cultural vector. Within cultures, people have developed and valued certain ideals that they support. They may or may not actually live up to these ideals, but there is a consensus that these ideals are inherently good.

Let's represent these ideals as cultural vectors and visualize them as an arrow. Vectors represent a magnitude and a direction. For our purposes,

---

[53] Freud, Sigmund. (1989). *The Freud Reader*

a cultural vector represents a cultural ideal. The arrow of the vector indicates a positive direction. In other words, the more the better. Let's look at an example. For many countries, one cultural vector is freedom. It is a guiding principle embodied in official documents.

Article I of the US Constitution:
Congress shall make no law respecting an establishment of religion or prohibiting the free exercise thereof; or abridging the **freedom** of speech, or of the press; or the right of the people peaceably to assemble, and to petition the Government for a redress of grievances.

Pledge of Allegiance
"I pledge allegiance to the Flag of the United States of America, and to the Republic for which it stands, one Nation under God, indivisible, with **liberty [freedom]** and justice for all."

The German constitution, adopted in May of 1949, includes the following five articles of basic rights. They fit very nicely into the idea of cultural vectors.
- Human Dignity
- Liberty
- Equality
- Faith, Religion, Conscience, Creed
- Expression

A translated version of the constitution of the People's Republic of China uses the word "freedom" 11 times and the word "right" or "rights" 39 times. [54] Included in the constitution is Article 35 which states, "Citizens of the People's Republic of China enjoy freedom of speech, of the press, of assembly, of association, of procession and of demonstration."

As I see it, there are three defining elements of a cultural vector:

---

[54] National People's Congress (NPC) of the People's Republic of China. (English version available 2006).
http://www.npc.gov.cn/zgrdw/englishnpc/Constitution/node_2825.htm

- It is embedded within the culture as a positive ideal. Everyone can recognize it. There is an emotional component that sometimes defies logic.
- The concept is actively and widely supported by key people and institutions. It is actively defended (although not necessarily practiced).
- Conceptually, the more of this vector, the better. Increasing the quality and reach of the ideal is desirable, although the practical application of the cultural vector can get quite confusing and vague.

In the U.S., "freedom" certainly meets the standard of the definition. The U.S. is billed as the "land of the free and the home of the brave." Those words are sung at major sporting events in "The Star-Spangled Banner." Have you ever heard a politician call for less freedom?

What are some other cultural vectors? Justice, equality, love, law and order, education, diversity, and independence to name a few. Notice the inherent conflicts among some of them. Different cultures promote different cultural vectors, and it's not all cut and dried.

In the U.S., there is a lot of praise for the principle of free speech. So how is it that people can be fired from their job for what they say, even when the words are shared outside of work in a personal private setting, say a restricted Facebook group?

It's true that the First Amendment protects people's right to say what they want. It's a deep-seated cultural vector. But in reality, the implementation is not so simple. Employers can set up a code of conduct that people must follow. Recently, employees of the U.S. Customs and Border Patrol were found to have posted some nasty messages and pictures in a private Facebook group regarding immigrants and asylum seekers. Based on the agency's code of conduct, employees of CBP aren't allowed to make "abusive, derisive, profane, or harassing statements or gestures" against people based on race, sex or national origin. Oops.

Furthermore, within each culture are conflicting cultural vectors. Let's take "order" as an example. By "order," I mean structure and organization that leads to people knowing their role, serving their purpose, and contributing to a peaceful coexistence. How does this square with the cultural vector of freedom? Here's one way that freedom and order work together. Governments are based on the idea that *free* and lawful elections provide an *orderly* transfer of power.

The cultural vector of order is manifested in other ways, with mixed results. Through the years, Confucianism has played a huge role in the structure of government and society in many parts of Asia. This structure provided order through a hierarchical form of government and specialized roles. There are benefits to this arrangement. For example, the formation of a scholarly class of people facilitated the discovery of new insights and the production of thoughtful writing and other works of art. In some ways, the structure reduced the destructive infighting and unproductive chaos of countries ruled by those with the most effective military might.

Yet with all the positive outcomes of this order, there are negative consequences, as well. A baby born into a society strictly based on Confucianism had a predetermined role fixed by its parents' ancestry. Dissent was stifled, and emotions were suppressed. Absent a meritocracy, where people earn their position, the production of output is undervalued, and dysfunctional behavior increases.

It's not hard to see the inherent conflict between the first ideal we discussed, freedom, and the ideals of structure and hierarchy. I have noticed that humans have trouble dealing with conflicting ideas. Psychologists call this cognitive dissonance. Holding two conflicting ideas in your head requires a lot of mental energy to resolve. Or a lot of rationalization.

F. Scott Fitzgerald described this challenge in his February 1936 essay, *The Crack-Up*: "The test of a first-rate intelligence is the ability to hold two opposed ideas in the mind at the same time, and still retain the ability to function. One should, for example, be able to see that things are hopeless, and yet be determined to make them otherwise."[55] He confessed his own struggles in this regard.

Oddly enough, it seems that this is where culture comes to the rescue for many people. In the melting pot of cultural ideals, there are conflicts. We've noticed that a culture may promote a vector that says, freedom is good, the more the better. And yet, structure (limits to freedom) are necessary ideals which preserve the status that people enjoy. The same

---

[55] Fitzgerald, F. Scott. *The Crack-Up.* p. 69

person that tears up singing about freedom in the Star-Spangled Banner on the Fourth of July, could be the same person who wants to build and strengthen a border wall.

In fact, cultural vectors are often in conflict. In physical science, when you combine two or more vectors via "vector addition," the result is a balance or compromise among them, often of intermediate magnitude in a new direction. The same is true with our concept of cultural vectors; the combination of cultural vectors demands a compromise.

The conflicts of cultural vectors can be resolved through a broader cultural framework that justifies their coexistence. When a set of people share a culture, they provide themselves with a way to validate an odd mix of opposing cultural vectors. A strong culture can justify this combination, resulting in the easing of cognitive dissonance. Cultures that have stood the test of time have a certain credibility. Members of such cultures can make the claim that their way of life works, that their particular mix of cultural vectors is a successful path to follow.

Call them cultural vectors or not, these kinds of ideals have existed throughout recorded history. Cultural vectors are a representation of cultural values. They bring people together for common causes. If a person can believe she is supporting and elevating a shared cultural value, her life has more meaning. Ideally, just as Saghi articulated, we are most satisfied when cultural values reflect our personal values.

I suggest that we take look at a controversial historic milestone in the U.S., the legalization of gay marriage, and how it applies to some of our concepts. In the year 1996, a Gallup poll found that 27% of the U.S. population supported same-sex marriage. In 2018, that figure had grown to 67%, a 40% increase over 22 years.[56] That's quite a rapid transition. I see multiple ways in which this transition reinforces some of our ideas.

Traditional cultures are breaking down. The practice, tradition, and (to many people) a sacred mandate that marriage is between a man and a woman has existed globally for thousands of years. Yet, over the course of a few years, public opinion shifted. One must acknowledge in this

---

[56] Gallup poll results on same-sex couples for 1996-2022 at https://news.gallup.com/poll/393197/same-sex-marriage-support-inches-new-high.aspx

103

instance the power of communication and the net effect to reach and influence the decision-makers and the general population. In 2013, Facebook reported on the response to a request by the Human Rights Campaign (HRC) that people change their Facebook profile pictures to a pink-on-red equal sign to show support for marriage equality. Analysis from the Facebook Data Science team noted that an estimated 2.7 million more Facebook users changed their profile images on Tuesday, March 26 (the day after the request was made) than the previous Tuesday.

The cultural vector of love was used to great effect. Proponents argued that people seeking marriage were simply expressing their love. The more love, the better. Who could stand against love and marriage? John Lewis, a leader of the civil rights movement said that "races don't fall in love, genders don't fall in love —people fall in love."[57]

Another strong message from proponents was that gay marriage would do no harm. Once people were convinced that this claim was true, many supported the right of the individual to make his own choice. I would argue that for most people, the idea of same-sex marriage did not become a widely supported cultural institution. Rather, it became an acceptable alternative in a world governed less by culture and more by personal choice.

Now we're getting to the heart of the problematic cultural condition. If broad-based cultures are losing their relevance and legitimacy, even cultural vectors could become weak, unsteady and conflicting signals. If people can't collectively agree on the meaning and desirability of important values, their journey could get solitary and confusing. All of which highlights the growing need for each person to proactively seek their individual values to guide their personal journey. In turn, these values help solidify an identity, the theme of the next voice.

---

[57] *The Atlanta Journal-Constitution*, June 26, 2015

Chapter 8

People want an Identity – Thai Voice

The primary religion of Thailand is Buddhism, but perhaps a passage from the Christian Bible best captures the essence of this interview. Matthew 5:13: "You are the salt of the earth, but if salt has lost its taste, how shall its saltiness be restored?" Is Thailand losing the very things that made it special?

Name: สุจินดา (Suchinda)
Self-described: Daughter, sister, normal person

(Born and lives in Bangkok, Thailand.)

Personal Identity

I am a daughter of my dad and my mom. I am who I am today because of them. I am a sister of my siblings. I have only one younger sister whom I see as part of my responsibility. I am a younger sister of my elder brother and sisters who helped raise me up after my father passed away.

I am just a normal person. I have always questioned myself what's wrong with me and why I couldn't be better. I remember well, one day after I asked myself why, something unexpected happened. My friend turned to me and just said that "nothing is wrong with you, you are OK. You are just a normal person. That's it." And it was actually an aha moment for me.

Cultural Identity

In the past I was able to say how Thailand was different from other countries. In the past, looking at this country, my country, my home country, I have always thought that our country is very peaceful. I don't know why, at that time because some uniqueness of our Thai people. For me, I have grown up surrounded by people in my family, my parents and my relatives, who compromised for me. We don't want to have conflict with others — this is my family, I don't know about others. That is what contributed importantly to our culture, to the peacefulness of our country at that time.

Now we have changes to our economy, I don't know maybe also because of the digital. We have more people from other countries and politics. Really difficult for me now, if you ask me, to identify the differences between Thailand and other countries.

Culture is the way we live life. I think the Buddhism religion contributes the big influence for Thailand. This is the attitude. We will pay back to people who are doing good to us. If you do something good to me, then I will try to find some way to do good back to you. Family is very important to us. When they grow up, I need to do good things back to them. Quite common to Asian countries.

For me, the biggest influence is my parents and Buddhism. When I look back, I am quite close to my mother and my father. My mother is a very generous person. They were very flexible, very compromising to other people. We lived in a neighborhood in a townhome. People were willing to share with others when they need something. Different today.

When you have more variety and diversity, you won't see a strong sense of the culture in a particular way. Because it is so diversified, the people become individual. Now it might be difficult for you to see the same behavior even compared to the people in the middle of the country.

Digital Influence

As I mentioned about digital. I think digital gives us a lot of things. Even though we are in Thailand, we can know about what happened in other countries. The biggest change for the next generation is that they live in the new digital world. This is something, the most important thing for me. My nieces, they still have the respect for the elders, but for the future generations, I don't know. Also, the pace of the machines, how things happen so quickly with the digital. When our behavior will change, then our lives, the culture will change.

Future of Culture

In the future, you might see some common culture across the world. Each generation will have a common culture. Depend on the generation. For value, we need to hold the important value that we have in our culture. Very important. Through parents and family, that is the most effective way to pass on values. If you want to continue it, you can teach them and let them practice it. But it will still be up to the next generation to decide what to do.

My Observations and Reflections

107

Lately, I've been looking at my screwups in life through the lens of the Second Noble Truth of Buddhism which states that all suffering is a result of Three Root Poisons: attachment (greed), aggression (hate), and ignorance (delusion). For me, the framework rings true. My mistakes and the associated suffering they caused now have an origin, a new perspective, and perhaps some warning signals. Could it be that my insight is like Suchinda's realization that she is a normal person? In both situations, nothing changed. We are simply looking at things differently.

When we look at our lives, we want to see something that sets us apart in a favorable way. Cultures are part of our identity and impact our relationships. When we decide to belong to a culture, we expect that engagement to enhance our standing with the people we care about. Suchinda laments that the culture of her country is no longer distinguishable from others. In her eyes, what made Thailand special was the value placed on supporting the needs of others. She has lost that sense of belonging to something with a higher purpose.

A currently popular personal goal is to become the best version of yourself. That requires knowing who you are, your limitations, and who you want to be. Becoming the best version of yourself doesn't exclude the support of others, but it does highlight the tension between someone's personal aspirations and a culture's shared values. In the case of Suchinda, everything that I know about her demonstrates her care for her family, fulfilling the strong sense of responsibility that she experienced as a child. It's her best version, her identity.

Suchinda talks about parents determining their most important values and passing them on to their children. She sees this process as well intentioned, but difficult. As she notes, the next generation will ultimately decide what to prioritize. The difference today is that the growing independence of youth in Thailand and elsewhere could lead to individualized pathways.

A well-defined culture establishes an identity, a means of building relationships, and a pathway. In this short interview, Suchinda openly acknowledges the importance of these elements in her life. Could you apply a name or short description of what you consider your culture to be? Does it set you apart in a way that is helpful?

The next section on identity will expand on the theme from this voice.

Identity

For one thing, being an Asian American, you look at your image first before adapting into an environment, to be accepted. (Hmong voice, Fwmtxaam)

In the last 20, 30 years, China has changed a lot. From my parents to my generation, to my daughter's generation. What I have learned from other countries has changed me a lot. (Chinese voice, 穎怡)

Identity is a critical part of our human development. It is an awareness of who we are, how we fit into the world, and our values. For the purposes of this discussion, I propose that the following components are vital elements of identity:

Biology and place — Everyone is born with biology and place. Both have significant implications. Your body has DNA and physical characteristics. Your birthplace will likely determine your citizenship. Each person strives to understand and manage elements of their identity. For some, this will involve working through racial and gender identities.

Capabilities — You are born with potential. How you are raised and what you choose to pursue will affect how well that potential is developed. A social identity will be formed.

Beliefs, values, and purpose —— These elements are developed and selected over time. You can decide to pick and choose from a buffet of options or order from a set menu, an established culture.

Alignment — Your identity is the most powerful and satisfying when the above three components of your identity are aligned and work well together.

Where does culture fit into identity? As we've defined it, culture is a broadly shared, multi-dimensional road map for life. Therefore, it is highly relevant to the "beliefs, values, and purpose" component and the alignment of those elements to the rest of your identity.

In this book, we've looked at cultures from various perspectives. Now we are zeroing in on how individuals accept a culture as part of who they are. That is critical because cultures without people are meaningless. If people do not align with a culture, that culture will not survive.

The inclusion of a culture within an identity might be conscious or unconscious. A culture becomes part of an identity when a person is motivated and consistent in following an established pattern of behavior and beliefs. People are motivated and consistent when this pattern of behavior and beliefs is aligned with who they are, how they fit into the world, and their values. As with everything else, there is a cost/benefit in adopting a culture.

Let me add another dimension to this identity discussion. For many people living in the increasingly complex world, they develop multiple approaches and personas that are used situationally. Someone can be a mother to three infants in the morning, a high-powered executive during the day, and a romantic partner in the evening. The next week this same person could be in another country where they assume an identity that better aligns with a different environment and expectations. This transformation is possible through the process of dissociation, the separation of various mental processes. People dissociate when they "filter out of consciousness many or most of their thoughts, feelings, and sensations registered at any moment."[58] This new level of complexity introduces another question. How can a single culture govern this growing assortment of identities resulting from a wide range of experiences?

In summary, an identity for humans is a magical blend of many elements: biology, place, capabilities, beliefs, values, and purpose. It's a developmental necessity. A culture can be a source or guide for many of these elements.

I find the following passages from *The Future of Capitalism* by Paul Collier relevant to our discussion.[59]

Society worked from 1945 to 1970 because it lived off a huge, invisible and unquantifiable asset that had been accumulated during the Second World War: a shared identity forged through a supreme and successful national effort.

Let me put that in slightly different words. The shared experience of a country working together to defend itself against a common enemy created an invisible and unquantifiable asset, a shared identity. Apparently, that shared identity enabled society to work well for the next 25 years. I'm going to make the short leap to say that this collective behavior, which lasted a generation, was indeed a culture. It took an extraordinary circumstance, a world war, to lead to the creation and staying power of this culture. Here's another quote from the same book.

Modern capitalism has the potential to lift us all to unprecedented prosperity, but it is morally bankrupt and on track for tragedy. … If capitalism is to work for everyone, it needs to be managed so as to deliver purpose as well as productivity.

---

[58] Carter, Rita. (2008). *Multiplicity: The New Science of Personality, Identity, and the Self.* p.62,79

[59] Indented quotes from Collier, Paul. (2018). *The Future of Capitalism: Facing the New Anxieties*

Apparently, this shared identity and drive that served the U.S. so well for many years no longer exists. According to the author, what seems to have replaced this identity is an overriding desire for productivity at the cost of purpose. If we compare this new identity to the identity components, we find capability, but the beliefs, values, and purpose are missing. In today's world, the persistence of a far reaching, uniform culture is becoming rare.

Many people are familiar with the generational identifiers such as Generation X, Generation Z, and millennials. The idea that generational environmental conditions will create shared characteristics and identifiable behavior patterns makes sense. It sounds vaguely like a culture, and it's consistent with our working definition. But many of the identified patterns of behavior for these categories seem to have a weak linkage to actual people. It's revealing that these groups are defined by birth years. It occurs to me that in the absence of true, identifiable cultures, establishing birth cut-offs was the only way to group people, give them a name and start assigning characteristics. If someone is born between 1981 and 1996, they are, by definition, a millennial. Whether this person acts or thinks the way millennials are defined is apparently irrelevant. Applying a stereotype becomes an easy exercise. "I wonder why she keeps changing her job. Ahh, no wonder, she's a millennial!"

Let's take one behavioral pattern from a study of megatrends by EuroMonitor International. The idea is that for Generation Z, conscious consumption has replaced conspicuous consumption.[60] To me, that sounds like this generation is more discriminating in its buying behavior and is more individualistic. A pattern, yes, but one that also supports the theory that personal values are driving behavior more than group dynamics.

All of which reinforces what I have proposed — that various conditions create culture, and that certain conditions are ideal for the growth of cultures. For example, companies can create an artificial environment that promotes their desired culture. Widespread environmental conditions that are a result of major forces (government

---

[60] Ha, Lan & Angus, Alison. (2021, March 15). New Strategies to Engage Millennials and Generation Z in Times of Uncertainty. *Euromonitor*

intervention or war for example) can also help create a strong shared identity or culture.

What I am also saying is that the reverse is true. Certain conditions work against the creation and stability of a cultural identity. It just so happens that many of these culture-resistant conditions are now present in our world, and the likelihood that they will be reversed is small. Hence, my concern.

Mental Health

People realize that events in their youth have lasting impacts on their identity in their adult lives. These events are both positive and negative. Bonding with loving parents is a good thing. Traumatic life events during childhood can be destructive and have lasting effects. Studies are finding apparent links between traumatic life events and the diagnosis later in life of borderline personality disorders (BPD).[61]

We've been talking about the connection between a person's identity and culture. How important for the mental health of people is the development of a healthy identity and functional culture? I can imagine these scenarios:

Problematic Situation	Possible Impact to Identity
Immigrants exposed in bits and pieces to conflicting cultures	Cultural experience disjointed, resulting in a lack of confidence in identity.
Exclusion due to race, handicap, or sexual orientation	Excluded from the predominant culture, they must look elsewhere for inclusion and identity.
Cults	Cults typically don't recognize individual needs and identities.

---

[61] Cattane N, Rossi R, Lanfredi M, Cattaneo A. (2017). Borderline personality disorder and childhood trauma: exploring the affected biological systems and mechanisms

Soldier returning from war	Identity built on experiences that others don't share; culture is inadequate to bridge the gaps.

Reading, writing, and math are taught in school. Where do people learn how to deal with cultural and identity issues? Perhaps the growing cultural challenges will help the powerful to recognize the very real crisis of mental illness in the world and respond accordingly. The growing use of alcohol and drugs is masking an epidemic of mental health issues that cultural change could either help or exacerbate.

I suspect that societal problems impacted by identity and culture are a factor in the following U.S. statistics:

- Between 1999 and 2019, the suicide death rate increased 33%. There were nearly 46,000 deaths by suicide in 2020, making it the 12th leading cause of death in the United States.[62]
- Suicide was the second leading cause of death for adolescents aged 15 to 19 years in 2015.[63]

Cultures play an important role in forming identities. In the absence of a functional and relevant culture connected to a healthy identity, people can struggle. When an individual is comfortable with their own cultural and personal identity, accepting and welcoming other cultures becomes easier.

---

[62] CDC WONDER, Multiple Cause of Death Files. (2019). America's Health Rankings analysis of CDC WONDER, Multiple Cause of Death Files, *United Health Foundation*, AmericasHealthRankings.org, accessed 2022.
[63] World Health Organization. (2018). LIVE LIFE: Preventing Suicide. *Department of Mental Health and Substance Abuse, World Health Organization*

Chapter 9

People rely on Trust – Swazi Voice

As we hear from Menzi, the homogenous and relatively small population of Eswatini (formerly Swaziland) has developed a family-oriented culture characterized by a high degree of trust. Imagine sending your children out into the neighborhood day after day, trusting your neighbors to feed and discipline them. Yet when it comes to romance, Menzi experiences uncertainty, secrecy, and gender-based roles for those seeking love.

Name: Menzi
Self-described: Gardener, pastor, cyclist
(Born and raised in Eswatini, Africa (Swaziland))

No One is a Stranger

I would say the culture of Eswatini is very family oriented. Culture in Eswatini comes from a sense of interdependency. In the family, you can count on them, and they can count on you.

When you meet someone, they will ask you questions to develop a sense of kinship. There is a sense of openness, of invitation. I might say, "I am Menzi from Tjaneni city," and they might say, "Oh, what is your father's name?" The purpose of the questions is to find a connection. Once someone has established some kind of connection, they can consider you a friend.

The sense that no one is a stranger is widely accepted across the country. If I were going for a walk and someone saw me, they might say, "Hello Dlamini," using the last name of the king of Eswatini as a complimentary greeting. This is a way of saying you are not a stranger, you are one of us, you are in the fold. People will ask about ancestors and current relatives to build trust. Although there is some prejudice and discrimination, if you meet someone from a different country and they speak the Swazi language, they also can claim the Swazi invitation. If they are hungry or thirsty, they can come up to someone's house, knock and ask for food or drink.

The environment there is different from the United States. Parents in Eswatini will let their children out in the neighborhood after dinner, and throughout the whole day. We believe people must trust each other, even with our kids. We give permission for others to give direction and to discipline our kids. With this trust established, parents can be confident that their children will be taken care of and fed. When challenges arise, they are discussed and dealt with.

U.S. Complexity

In the U.S. at college, the biggest challenge for me was to determine whether a person considered me a friend. In our culture, we assume almost everyone we meet is a friend. When you approach someone, most people will smile. Right? And from college students, that's a three-second smile. I might say, "Hello, how are you doing?" as an invitation to engage, but they have already passed. In our Eswatini culture, greeting someone implies that you really want to know how they are. I had to appreciate the differences and navigate that.

I might meet someone at the library and have a talk, and we talk about significant things. Then the next day, I see this person, they might act like they don't know me. Because of our discussion, I had already considered him or her as a friend.

Like and Love

When it comes to dating, Swazis would be considered too forward. When you meet a woman, there is no difference between like and love. In our language, there is only one word that covers both situations, tsandza. The words "I love you" and "I like you" are both represented by a one-word sentence, ngiyakutsandza. After a conversation of 30 minutes, one might say to a woman that you like her. But what you are essentially saying is "I love you" and hope to hear the same back. Also, you are not able to directly ask her for a date. All you can do is say that I will be in this location (by the river) at this time (sunset) and wait for her. For the woman, there is an issue. The parents want the daughter to get married, but they don't want her to go on a date. There is a bit of secrecy. You can only introduce your partner to your parents when ready and committed to marriage.

There can be a context in which people are open to play (engage) even if the woman doesn't necessarily want to have a date. You can continue for three months. The funny thing is that the man expects the woman to have a change of heart. It's not so much that she will decide that the man is perfect for her, it is more that he believes that he can be persuasive. The woman could be saying that "I don't like you," but you may be thinking that the woman is playing hard to get. You may bring her flowers and other gifts and she may never say yes. It's an interesting dance. When you translate this behavior to America, you could be considered too forward, or you could be accused of harassing the woman.

Media Impact

The media has influenced differences in the generations. I grew up listening to U.S. music. Now people can be listening to something from anywhere. Earlier generations tended to be more conservative in nature. This conservative nature doesn't necessarily come with hate, just a desire to preserve culture and tradition. Sometimes you can get a resistance to Westernization, which may come from the trauma of colonization, something the older generation has experienced. Education has influenced us as well. Young people tend to be more Western because they are exposed to more things.

Waves of Leadership

If you live in Swaziland, you might feel like the options are not ideal. For people who are older, they have experienced a peace enforced by the soldiers and tight regulations. Today, it is less peaceful with more exposure to the world and less control. There are more strikes; it almost feels like a civil war. To older people, it feels like we have fewer opportunities than before. Hospitals used to give you free medicine, now you must pay and it may not be available. For young people, the world is our oyster. We have more access to information and opportunities.

With colonization, there is a pressure to conform. As a former British colony, we already had that. We were expected to put on a suit and a tie. Elders in school put pressure on the kids to be more Western-like. For example, they care how you comb your hair. This behavior can put down what is traditional Swaziland. It happens because sometimes the values are in conflict. The access to Western media can make the situation worse.

Culture of Kinship

I often think about who I am now and how maybe my culture prepared me for that. I talked about this culture of kinship with others. I often think that in comparison to the U.S., I was so fortunate. How lucky I was to grow up in a place where the parents didn't need to worry about the kids. Nearly every adult has the best interest in mind for you, even if they punish you for something. If something was happening at home, even domestic violence, as a child you can run to the neighbors and say, trouble, trouble at home. The neighbors will help you, for sure, for sure. That sense of acceptance and community has helped prepare me for my role, even though it can lead to misunderstanding in the United States. I can't overemphasize how much it has helped me in terms of my ministry.

My Observations and Reflections

What does it take for someone to jump out of a plane with a parachute? Trust. Trust in the trainer, the equipment, and yourself. That trust is built on familiarity, experience, and relationships. You might not know the trainer personally, but your close trusted friend can speak for her.

For Menzi, his trust in the neighborhood was built on years of experience and, no doubt, the testimony of people he has come to trust. Even in his relationships with women, there was a shared recognition of the game to be played, with all its uncertainly and risks. He has relied on this sense of trust as he moved to the U.S., went to school here, and eventually became a pastor. Lacking a strong foundational community like that of Eswatini, he has leveraged his past, adjusted his approach, and built a meaningful life.

Relationships

Even now, if a traditional Hmong man wants to marry my daughter, I will expect a dowry to show respect. The money is not to buy, but to show respect for the people involved. (Laotian voice, Keo)

Learning how to be a friend is a very culturally sensitive exercise, learned over time. And for the young, it changes from one year to the next. Friendship in middle school has different nuances and characteristics than in high school. A middle school friend gave her buddy a friendship bracelet she made in her favorite color. But two years later in high school, she gives her a fist bump. Different rules for different schools. And when those rules are broken, peer pressure takes over and sets people straight, or tries to.

Animals seem to have a much easier time. They have strong instincts that guide them. Moose and elk have dramatic battles for females during rutting season that are generally ritualized. Less physical are canyon bats and harvest mice that sing to their intended partners. Male stag beetles will use their large jaws to throw an opponent off a rotting tree, their typical breeding ground. While the competitor is climbing back, the remaining stag beetle mates with the available female. [64]

For something as complicated and nuanced as a friendship, there needs to be a very robust means of communicating values, rituals, and feelings. In the U.S., this communication may have occurred in the girls' bathroom, the boys' locker room, or at the mall. Now it's digital as well. Digital capabilities bring people together regardless of their location. People can have a wider range of contacts, and they are exposed to a broader range of behaviors. Furthermore, cultures adapt, evolve, and homogenize when they intersect.

The results of these communications are mixed. People who are exposed to very different cultures gain only a superficial understanding of them, even when they think otherwise. It takes a lifetime and special context to know and live a culture. That's why when someone begins to take on attributes of a culture where they don't belong, people consider it an appropriation.

Relationships provide a sense of uniqueness that people desire. In a relationship, you are special. Let's take an interesting example of connectedness, one that claims to revolutionize relationships: online dating.

Chances are pretty good that you know someone who has used online dating services, whether they admit it or not. According to the Pew Research Center (2019), 30% of U.S. adults say they have used a dating site or app. [65]

In some ways, the online dating process makes perfect sense. Get access to data, process, categorize and prioritize. That's how good decisions are made. But then there's the human factor. Are people honest in building their profile? Roughly seven in 10 online daters believe it is very common for those who use these platforms to lie to appear more desirable. Do people know what they want or need? Are people

---

[64] Dinets, Vladimir. *Wildlife Spectacles: Mass Migrations, Mating Rituals, and Other Fascinating Animal Behaviors*. (2016)

[65] The online dating findings included here come from a nationally representative survey of 4,860 U.S. adults conducted online Oct. 16 to 28, 2019, using Pew Research Center's American Trends Panel. https://www.pewresearch.org/internet/2020/02/06/the-virtues-and-downsides-of-online-dating/

courageous enough to share their true needs and values? And finally, even with all that data, do people make the right dating choice?

We've covered how people tend to categorize or pigeonhole others based on general characteristics. My guess is that when people swipe left on a profile after two seconds, they are basing their decision on appearance and assumptions alone.

In the U.S., 12% of adults say they have married or entered into a committed relationship with someone that they first met through a dating site or app. That's an 18% gap between the total users (30%) and successful users. Americans who have used a dating site or app in the past year said the experience left them feeling more frustrated (45%) than hopeful (28%). Roughly three in 10 online dating users said someone they met through a dating site or app continued to contact them after they said they were not interested (37%), sent them a sexually explicit message or image they didn't ask for (35%), or called them an offensive name (28%).[66] So, what's the deal? You probably have your own theory for the apparent failures of online dating, but my guess is that many of the complications come from a lack of trust. This lack of trust can result from a misunderstanding of expectations.

Cultures are like icebergs. Many of the cultural components are invisible, underwater. Someone can see physical differences, but the inner value system, expectations and patterns of interaction are harder to discern. Without a degree of trust, people will not expose their inner selves.

I'm going to play it safe here. Love, marriage, and friendship — all three are complex. I just want to make a couple points. There are an incredible number of important decisions to be made in a close personal relationship, and there are tremendous opportunities for misunderstandings. People make large investments in the people they care about. I believe that most people, based on their own relationships, would agree. The responsibility of any culture then is to provide behavioral guidelines. While many of these cultural guidelines may be ill-founded, they enable people to have meaningful relationships by establishing the rules of the road. People make progress when they can correctly interpret

---

[66] Anderson, M., Vogels, E. A., & Turner, E. (2020, February 6). The Virtues and Downsides of Online Dating. *Pew Research Center*

the actions of others and have a means to communicate their own feelings. When they have success interpreting and communicating, they build trust with each other. Just like Menzi experienced as a child.

Within a shared culture, the workings of values and decision-making are similar, which allows people to interact efficiently. When there are two different cultures interacting, one can suppose that extended and deep interaction will be problematic unless people know how to handle the differences.

Now think about the world we are headed toward. People are exposed to a wider variety of cultures, many of which are going through change. Given the human tendency to mask their true feelings, how in the world do we cope?

Growing up, my family rarely shared our feelings. To illustrate how impersonal we could get, consider that among us brothers, we did not call each other by our first name or even by an endearing nickname. We used our initials. Consequently, I was MB, my older brother SB and my parents AB and JB. Odd, yes, but it represented the nature of our relationships at that time.[67]

The world is in transition. When people question pre-conceived assumptions of the past and really get to know others for who they are, it's a better world. Let me give a dramatic example from the past. In the Hmong community, courtship was quite limited. In Asia, Hmong people lived in small villages that were isolated from each other.[68] One cultural practice was for a man to express his desire for a woman to his family, who would then kidnap her. She would be held by the man's family while a negotiation for the marriage was held between the two families.

I'm sure that in the past there were reasons for this kind of practice to exist, and I know that I am missing important details. But in the light of modern values, this arrangement would be most disturbing and illegal if practiced in the U.S, where many Hmong now live. There appear to be cultural assumptions that the man is better able to make the marriage

---

[67] My younger brother's initials presented a bit of a problem. TB brings to mind tuberculosis, an unpleasant image. My older brother reversed the initials to BT, and we pronounced his nickname "Beat." Problem solved.

[68] We will talk about the courtship of ball tossing in the Hmong community in a later chapter.

decision and that kidnapping is justified to force negotiations. Maybe there was another assumption that prolonged courtship was not practical and that the most important outcome in the lives of Hmong at that time was procreation and not happiness. Regardless, I'm willing to guess that the leadership of the Hmong community was male dominated. Would you agree that having both male and female input to the marriage decision could make for a higher percentage of happy and compatible couples?

Do you see where I am headed? Love and marriage are critically important to a population and typically have cultural guidelines. These guidelines often do not have universal application and could be established for the wrong reasons. Rethinking historical assumptions and moving to a world where people are respected and understood as individuals seems like a good thing.

People will need tools and time to do the job. Think about insights gleaned from Myers Briggs and Discover, personality assessments that help people understand some of the hidden workings of their teammates. Cultural assumptions are shortcuts, and we know they are increasingly off the mark. There is no substitute for building an environment of trust to get people to share their true self.

Chapter 10

People are shaped by their Environment
Korean Voice

By sharing his own generational experience, Jinho gives a touching, personal description of how life has changed in Korea.

Name: 진호 (Jinho)
Self-description: I am who I am, a man who wants to live happily and live the truth.
(Born and living in South Korea.)

My hometown is located in the south part of Korea. I lived there for one third of my life, two thirds of my life in Seoul. I was the only son, with one younger sister.

Korean Culture of my Childhood

People of my age and my father's age are quite unique because we could experience many different Korean cultures. When I was a child, at that time, my grandmother's living situation in the country was like that of 500 years ago.

When I was born in Korea, the country was quite poor. We lived together in a small room with my parents when I was 5 or 6 years old, but now I have a big house and three cars. When I was young, even though we were very poor, we didn't think that we were poor, because all over my neighborhood they were in the same situation.

When I was in middle school, my grandmother lived with us in our house. She really liked me, and it makes sense. I am the only son, and my father was also the only son. All the people liked the son. I was a lovely child for my grandmother. I received unconditional love.

My grandmother did not talk very much about her history. At the time she was young, Korea had trouble with the Korean War and the colonization period. At that time, it was very difficult, so she didn't like to talk about that period.

Individual vs. Group

The culture that I experienced as a child is different than the culture of today. When I was a child, Korean culture would focus on the union of the people rather than the individual. Our country has had a sad history, like being occupied by Japan, and attacked by many countries. Because of that, we believed it was the right thing to sacrifice ourselves for our family, our hometown and our country.

Compared to when I was a child, the individual is more important now. We are no longer asked to sacrifice for the union. Everyone sticks to their own business. Only when I am happy, I can support my family;

if I am not happy, I can't support my family. It is quite a big change in the way of thinking.

I am not sure how the changes came about. That kind of culture is affected by the other countries, maybe Europe or America. Because in oriental culture, it only focuses on the union, not the individual. In Europe or America, we could know that the individual is more important.

Cultural change is related to economic change. When I was a child, it was quite a poor country. When my father was born in this country, the per capita GDP was $100 or $200 U.S. dollar. At the time I was born, the GDP was $2,000 U.S. dollar, nowadays our GDP is more than $30,000. So now we don't worry about food, clothes or house anymore. When we were so poor, someone needed to sacrifice for another person, for the family.

Ten years ago, most Korean people preferred a son, but lately most of the people prefer the daughter. We normally have a service each year to honor the ancestors on the date of their death and only sons can have that service. But now many people don't take the time for that service.

Digital Perceptions

I think that social media has some effect on the culture. I have had some time to study how it affects our lives. Some are good, and some are bad. Many people have social media now and they are easily engaged with other people. Social media affects some things for the people, for example, everyone wants to show in the social media how they are very happy. People look at others' posts and they think that everyone is happy except for me.

I like the traveling, so I would post my traveling activity. One of my friends told me he is stressed out when he sees my reporting. He is a very rich man, a doctor, but he has no time to travel. So, he feels some stress when he sees my posts with the travel. So, I have stopped my social posting, six months ago.

Culture Today and in the Future

Many people say that in previous years we were happier than now because even though we enjoy a very good economy these days, we have no leisure time to enjoy with our family. When I was living in the small house as a boy, we would do lots of talking.

Today, many of my friends who work in the Korean company don't have time to talk with their family. Even when they have free time, their mind is tied up with some difficulty in the work.

The unions in Korea are trying to establish a work week of 52 hours maximum. Many people are trying to destroy the hierarchical nature in Korea. Even in my company, we changed our title to be the same for all the employees. It is beginning to change the hierarchy.

Recently, I attended a lecture concerning trends and the prediction is that people will become even more individualistic. The Korean birth rate is very low and lots of Korean people today do not marry. Even my daughters say that they don't want to marry.

I think people will be even more individualistic in the future. When I was a child, we follow good people's lives. But the people don't do that today. Their own circle is what is important, and they don't need someone to follow. They have their own destination.

My Observations and Reflections

I find Jinho's story particularly touching. The generational changes in Korea are dramatic and Jinho makes them personal.

The isolated and impoverished world of many Koreans of only a generation or two ago has become globally connected and economically strong. It's no wonder that the newest generation looks to itself for enlightenment more than to their parents. The expectations and pathways to success have changed with the environment. Cultures are shaped by the ecosystems in which they exist.

In terms of observations, I consider the last paragraph of Jinho's interview to be an excellent subject for contemplation. Are we all headed to the point where a circle of friends replaces the need for a passed-down culture? With the information and options available, are people able to define their own set of guidelines independently? Or will the limited experience of that circle of friends only serve to guide them through familiar territory?

North Korean Cultural Transformation

Of all the countries in the world, why focus on Korea? With North and South Korea, we have an ideal social environment to test some theories. We have a country that was split into two different pieces, one completely isolated from the other. This allows us to track the different cultural outcomes over many years under different environmental conditions.

The unfortunate split of the country began at the end of World War II in 1945. After a series of bloody encounters, the Korean War began in 1950. While a peace treaty was never signed, the Korea Armistice Agreement, establishing the border between North and South Korea, was enacted in 1953.

The whole of Korea also provides an example of a country that's existed for thousands of years with a strong, rich culture, but has experienced profound change in the last 50 years.

Isolation

More and more shared knowledge exists today, yet each person's experiences and perspectives are increasingly unique. With this diversity, forming and internalizing common actions and beliefs becomes more challenging.

Strong cultures can develop when an isolated set of people faces similar challenges and adopts common strategies for facing challenges and meeting needs. But today, with notable exceptions, people are no longer isolated. With increased information at their disposal, people are free to make independent decisions on how to proceed.

Odd as it might seem, in today's hyper-connected world, artificially created isolation and censorship do still exist. This isolation can be a rich environment for the development of a strong culture. Remember these elements from our definition of culture and how it develops:

"shared experiences over **time"**
"response to **needs** and **widely accepted assumptions."**

What better way to ensure that people share similar experiences over time than to severely restrict behavior and institutions? With dedicated effort, communications can be controlled. Enforced loyalty and extreme punishment help to ensure compliance. On top of that, a government could put most people in a position where they are constantly dependent on it for the basic needs of food and shelter.

In a nutshell, I've just described the world of North Korea. Everyone there is forced to pledge allegiance to the leader, who is treated like a god. There is one legal source of information, the government. Commerce is illegal, although limited black markets are tolerated somewhat because they bring in foreign currency.

In each residence, families are required to keep pristine framed pictures of the present and past leaders of North Korea on the wall. Each home also includes a loudspeaker for daily broadcasts of patriotic songs and propaganda. Radios and TVs are altered so that only the officially sanctioned state broadcasts are available.

Any negative talk about the government can lead to arrest and imprisonment in cruel work camps. Escaping the country will lead to punishment of the remaining relatives. This is one of the most restricted environments in the world today.

As noted earlier, the separation of the two Koreas began in 1945 at the end of World War II. The war between the two Koreas was five years later, 1950-1953. It wasn't long before it became clear that North and South Korea would take two very different paths.

This rigid separation provides a dramatic demonstration of the forces influencing culture. In South Korea, the eventual awakening of commercialization and democratic rule brought a higher standard of living, but also led to a rapid dismantling of a culture that was shaped by Confucius thousands of years ago. We'll cover the evolution of South Korea later. For now, let's investigate the cultural implications of the repressed North.

Over the years, the North became more and more isolated as the government cut off communications from most of the world. At the same time, Korean families were split up by an impassible border. This extreme isolation meant there were few external inputs into the culture, and the rules imposed on people's behavior were exceedingly rigid.

The government of North Korea goes to great lengths to block out conflicting lifestyles. Watching a DVD of a U.S. television show or movie is strictly prohibited and strongly punished. Still, North Koreans hungry for a glimpse of the outside world will occasionally block out their windows to view an illegal copy in secret.

One might think that seeing an American show would expose the lies about conditions in the U.S., but no. People are so blinded by the propaganda and claims that conditions in North Korea are vastly superior to anywhere else in the world that they consider the shows to be fantasy.

I do admire the determination and resourcefulness of the people to see the outside world. When suspicions are raised that someone is watching illegal content, the state police will cut off the electricity to the home, thereby trapping the contraband VCR tape or DVD in the machine. While you might think this presents a hopeless situation, people have devised a creative escape. They will quickly swap out the VCR or DVD player with an old one.[69]

I hope that you are beginning to get the picture of everyday life there. Imagine an environment where your status depended on the perception of your family's past dedication to the principles of the ruling party. Each family is assigned a caste or "songbun." Even a family that has worked for years to build a good songbun could lose all its gains by breaking a simple rule.

---

[69] Park, Yeonmi. (2015). In Order to Live: *A North Korean Girl's Journey to Freedom.*

People are shaped by their Environment

People of North Korea are divided by the government into three main groups.[70] The highest ranking is made up of people whose ancestors have showed their loyalty to the current government, who served as revolutionaries for the North. The next ranking includes those who had lived in the south or were merchants or intellectuals. The lowest class, considered to be "hostile," includes those who, based on their occupation or behavior, have proved themselves to be enemies of the state. Former landowners, capitalists, Christians, families of political prisoners and others make up this group. The persecution of Christians in North Korea is considered to be the most severe in the world.

Most of the people have shared a similar experience, with little external exposure and a shared struggle to follow the rules and survive. People have very few decisions to make as the state controls their lives. In the information vacuum, they were told, and many believed, that their country was the best in the world, and they are most fortunate to live there.

What kind of culture comes out of this isolated and remarkably controlled environment? A very structured one. In a serious environment like this one, variations from the norm don't just bring about social pressure, they can result in death. However, there's a risk for such an extreme and one-sided culture. Of the 178 countries rated, North Korea is the 32nd most vulnerable country for conflict or collapse, according to the 2022 Fragile States Index.[71]

Let's make clear that many people in North Korea have lived a difficult life, especially when food was scarce. Many starved. However, I believe that the culture that was formed in those trying conditions helped people deal with the difficult environment. This culture, while based on lies, helped people make sense of the world they lived in.

The information about North Korea is limited. But based on what we have available, we know the environment has produced some unusual characteristics. People with power not only have a disproportionate influence over a culture, but they also have a strong personal interest in what cultures support.

---

[70] Ibid.

[71] Fragile States Index. (2022). *The Fund for Peace*. https://fragilestatesindex.org/global-data/

- Romantic love has little place in the culture. Even holding someone's hand in public is highly unusual.
- Family is vitally important. Outside of the family, there is little trust. People are rewarded by the government for spying on others and reporting their misbehavior.
- Upward mobility is virtually non-existent. Downward mobility is a threat that everyone faces.
- There is no tolerance of religion, but worship of the "great leader" is mandatory.
- Advanced education is for the privileged few, determined by the state.

In some ways, kids in this environment are just like kids around the world. They grow up considering that their reality is the way things are for everyone. They don't have another credible reference point. North Koreans who have escaped the country and made their way to South Korea have confirmed this condition. The poverty and starvation they experienced in North Korea were the prevailing conditions and were not considered unusual. They were told that they were very fortunate to live in North Korea, where conditions are much better than elsewhere. Furthermore, they were lucky to be born into a country with a powerful leader and state to watch over them and protect them from the American aggressors.

That's how cultures are passed on to new generations. Children look to their parents and others close to them to explain the world. Parents teach them simplified and lofty ideals. Conditions are controlled to teach them the benefits of fitting in and following the rules. Appropriate behavior is rewarded, inappropriate behavior is corrected or punished. Just go to a playground in a middle-class neighborhood in the U.S. and listen.

- Wait your turn please, she was there first.
- The slide is there for everyone, we need to share.
- That ball is not yours, please leave it alone.

Parents at the playground might not know each other, but they know the general rules by which interaction is governed. The playground is not a jungle. "Being there first" affords some benefit. "Taking turns" is how community property is shared. Not everything is communal, so private property must be respected. Of course, the messaging could be quite different somewhere else.

In most of today's world, kids are increasingly exposed to alternate ideas and different parts of the world. Many begin surfing the Internet or exploring YouTube at an early age. But not in North Korea. Even if their parents begin to see through the distortions of the state, they are afraid to share their concerns with their kids. If the child goes to school and innocently repeats some of these non-conforming ideas, the parents will likely face terrible consequences.

Culture is a shared interface between people and the day-to-day reality that they face. It is how people make sense of their surroundings and collectively deal with them. It's also the understanding of how people interact with each other. In the case of North Korea, the reality they face is a harsh one, so the culture needs to shape itself accordingly.

Take the case of romantic love. One might think that romantic love is biologically hardwired to the human psyche, but the conditions on the ground in North Korea are not compatible with romance. Mi-ran of North Korea admitted, "It took us three years to hold hands. Another six to kiss." [72] Marrying outside of your social standing can be very detrimental. Often, marriages are arranged. The lack of disposable wealth limits the ability to pamper a partner. In addition, any role models of a romantic couple are absent, given all media is directed toward serving the state. Without guidance, means, and support, romantic behavior can't survive.

Therefore, the culture reflects accommodations dictated by the harsh conditions. Because the conditions are widespread and stable, more "practical" behavior toward the opposite sex becomes a cultural norm across the population.

Of course, North Korea is not the only country to have experienced a cultural distain for physical intimacy, with the government playing a big part. From 1949, when the People's Republic of China was born, to when it opened up in 1980, there was not a single kiss in a China-mainland movie. Finally, in the 1979 feature, *The Thrill of Life*, there was a near kiss

---

[72] Demick, Barbara. (2010). *Nothing to Envy: Ordinary Lives in North Korea*

that disappointed many audiences. As the lovers were about to consummate their kiss, the mother-in-law broke up the action. You can imagine the anticipation of the audience, many of whom had never seen an on-screen kiss. Alas, they would need to wait another year.

China was able to witness true romance in a beautiful setting in 1980's *Romance on Lushan Mountain*. For many Chinese, this movie was a lesson in how two people in love can express their feelings in a relationship. For many people in the Western world, to imagine a world without romantic love would be challenging. But for Chinese audiences, they were thrilled or perhaps shocked when American born and raised Zhou Yun (Zhang Yu) gave a peck on the cheek to her shy, naive boyfriend, the son of a senior general of the Chinese Communist Party (Guo KaiMin).[73]

How quickly things change. While North Korea used extraordinary means to prevent the practice of love and romance, China now regularly screens plenty of romantic American movies and their own moviemaking prowess continues to grow — proving again, the power of enhanced global communication and the Net Effect.

Here's a fascinating example from a topic we've already touched on briefly. In large part due to the teachings of Confucius, cultures in Asia began to separate into hierarchies. I am simplifying things here, but in general they developed a ruling class, an academic class, and a common working class.

Democracy proponents might think of these different classes as a bad thing, but the underlying structure sure beats having warring clans constantly killing each other in fights for dominance. Some would argue that ruling and academic classes were necessary to apply sufficient time, study, and debate on important governing decisions and idea creation. This new class order did provide some stability and opportunity for advancement in civilization.

As with most situations, there's a negative side as well. When ruling classes became power hungry and academics became lazy, the structure lost its value. The working class was stuck at the bottom, so their motivation was stifled. But the culture carried on, because the people at the top had the influence to keep things going in their favor. Not only

---

[73] Groundbreaking Chinese movies reviewed by Yi, Ziyi. (Nov 2019). Sex, Lips, and Videotape. *News China*

that, at times they took Confucianism to extremes, and used cruel punishment to maintain the status quo. For one dynasty, a fixed sequence of cutting off body parts was the way it dealt with repeat offenders. Having said this, I am going to take the liberty to expand the definition of culture to include these realities.

- Culture provides people with a means to cope with and to survive their shared conditions.
- Culture is naturally shaped by social pressure, but it can also be corrupted and manipulated for selfish gain.

By examining an isolated part of the world, North Korea, we've revealed how the environment shapes a way of life. In this case, the government plays an oversized role in defining and overseeing the boundaries of life there.

Enforcing a uniform culture is risky. If the government falls, people are left with little to guide them. This will be the case for North Korea and Iran as it has been for other long-standing oppressive regimes. Consider the chaos that Libya endured once Khadafy and his government were eliminated.

Imagine how hard it would be to relate to someone from North Korea without understanding the challenging circumstances of life there. Given the diversity of people and backgrounds in most of the world today, patience and listening are vitally important to building and sustaining relationships.

Now let's move on to the broader Korean experience, where one of the strongest and longest lasting cultures has been rapidly changing and, some might say, disappearing.

South Korean Cultural Transformation

Believe it or not, right after the split of Korea, North Korea did better economically than South Korea. It had been the richer and more industrialized part of the country, and it received lots of monetary support from the Soviet Union after the end of the Korean war. The South based its economy on agriculture and had suffered greatly during the invasion of the North. The South also had troubles with corruption in the government led by the U.S.-installed anti-communist leader, Syngman Rhee.

Eventually the South became a profitable manufacturing center, while the highly restricted and centrally planned economy of the North began to falter. The troubles for the North greatly intensified with the breakup of the Soviet Union and the loss of its financial support. Feeding the population became difficult and many in North Korea starved. Currently, the GDP per capita in South Korea is about 40 times that of the North.

Prior to the split into North and South Korea, Korea was similar in many ways. As mentioned earlier, much of Asia was greatly influenced by Confucianism. Beginning around the time of Christ, Confucianism blended with Shamanism in Korea to create a very distinct and strong culture. This culture developed many different cultural characteristics over time that dominated Korean lives and lasted into the 20th century.

The hierarchical nature of Confucian society and the power of the ruling class kept this culture in place. Korea's isolated geographic location was also a factor. While not an island, Korea is a peninsula in the Pacific Ocean, bordered only by China and a thin strip of Russia, with Japan their nearby neighbor. In Korea's history, many of the people preferred that Korea remain a very separate and homogeneous people. It is only in the last couple of generations that the attitude has changed. Today, most of the Koreans under 35 want to increase communication with people of other countries. Their sense of identity as a Korean people is not as strong.

With the infusion of democratic principles and the economic success of South Korea, many of these cultural qualities have been altered. The relatively rapid changes in Korean society are interesting to us because they strongly support our theory that cultures of the world are being impacted due to global trends. You will see our point as we investigate a few of the interesting cultural rules and behaviors within the mind-map of Korea.

Beliefs and practices that have existed for hundreds of years have been eliminated or changed. For example, South Korea became the fastest growing country for new Christian followers. In Seoul, the Christian cross became a dominant fixture of the city's scenery.

In some ways, Korea is like many other countries. Some of the cultural heritage exists only in museums, exhibits or tourist attractions. It is not unusual for dress or customs to get lots of attention from those interested in a country's culture. But it's the internal beliefs, language, and interpersonal interaction that are more significant and enduring, but less visible.

I find the proverbs of a county very enlightening. They give insight to a country's focus and wisdom. Here are a few from Korea. [74]

남의 떡이 더 크게 보인다
"The other person's rice cake looks bigger."
Someone else's situation always looks better.

그림의 떡이다

---

[74] Holt, Daniel D. & Holt, Grace Massey. (1988). *Korean at a Glance*

"Rice cakes in a picture."
To long for something but be unable to have it.

둘이 먹다가 한 사람 죽어도 모른다
"When two are eating, one could die and the other wouldn't notice."
When eating a delicious meal, we are not conscious of anything else.

수박 겉 핥기
"Licking the outside of a watermelon."
Just scratching the surface, not dealing with something in depth.

빈 수레가 더 요란하다
"An empty pushcart makes more noise."
The most talkative people are often those who know the least.

우물안 개구리
"A frog in a well."
Used to describe someone who lacks vision or a broad perspective.

Notice the attention on common concerns, such as food and relationships. If one were to substitute a word or two, the sayings would fit in nicely in Western countries. For example, "dessert" could be used for "rice cake." A "wheelbarrow" would work well for "pushcart." I believe that "a frog in a well" needs no revision, especially for those familiar with the story of a frog who lived at the bottom of the well and believed what he experienced was the entire world.

Sayings endure because they resonate with many people in a variety of situations, build off common elements, and ring true. The same situation exists for many beliefs and cultural vectors. If these sayings are so familiar to Western thought, what makes Korea unique and interesting? Check out this saying:

작은 고추가 맵다
"A small pepper is hot."
Small people have the fortitude and toughness to accomplish things.

Here lies evidence of the Korean spirit and ability to endure hardship and persevere. There has been plenty of adversity for Korea over the years. Korea has been invaded many times and occupied multiple times, but has never initiated a war with another country. Most recently, it was occupied by Japan from 1910 to 1945.

We've stated that Korea's culture had many common elements for hundreds of years due to the long-term dominance of a Confucian mindset. This mindset led to a suppression of personal expression that seems to have had a widespread effect on the personality of many Koreans. In fact, in pre-modern Korea, the direct, public expression of emotions (including love) was considered immoral. It was a punishable offense. Why? Because Confucian thought believed that emotions were disruptive to the harmony of society.

It has been said that harmony has been the overriding goal of Korean society. Remember our discussion of cultural vectors? They are actively supported, positive ideals embedded within a culture, and the more, the better. I think it is safe to assume that for much of Korea's history, societal harmony could be called a primary cultural vector.

Harmony sounds like a good outcome, doesn't it? But what price needs to be paid for harmony to prevail? With such universal acceptance and obedience to the ideal of harmony, other elements of Korean life suffered. While I know there are many factors to consider, the suicide rates of both North and South Korea are the highest for any country, at over three times the rate of the U.S. To get an idea of how quickly long-held Korean cultural elements are fading, let's examine some of the unique aspects of Korean culture.

It was General Song Gye Yi, the founder of the Chosen dynasty in 1392, who made neo-Confucianism the state ideology and the state religion. This effectively reinstated the philosophy of kolpum, a hierarchical ranking system based on ancestry that started during the golden age of the Shilla period. Interestingly, the ancestry was based on "bone ranks," rather than the concept of blood lines used elsewhere in the world. It follows that the highest class consisted of the song gol or "sacred bones." The royal family were identified as the chin gol or "true bones."[75]

Kolpum endured for centuries. Almost 500 years passed before it started to break down. When the Japanese annexed Korea in 1910, they ended the practice, but the related concept of filial piety, the virtue of respect for one's parents and ancestors, still dominated Korean society.

Here is where it gets very interesting. It was the 1970s when the cultural mindset of kolpum and associated filial piety took a hard fall. As Korea's interaction with other countries and cultures increased, the absolute belief in ancestor worship diminished. Currently, the rites of ancestor worship are still practiced by more traditional families, more as a ritual. The societal concept of the two-generation family, the hakgajok, began to dominate thinking.

This shift has quickly led to a decrease in the centuries-old customs of respecting parents and maintaining close familial bonds.

The crucial takeaway is that the basic social fabric of ancestor worship and filial piety that organized Korean society and families endured for many centuries. Yet the increased interaction with other cultures over a short period of 60 years has greatly reshaped Korean thinking and family life. The two-generation or nuclear family is becoming the new norm. The interaction within that family has been significantly altered. I consider this very significant in multiple ways:

- The speed of change increased as mobility and communication expanded across cultural boundaries.
- The population moved closer toward a global standard.
- The new structures had a comparative lack of cultural guidance.

We haven't adequately considered the cost of maintaining extreme harmony mentioned earlier. What is the price to be paid for an outward appearance of harmony forced upon a population? Why is this important? It establishes the reality that cultural standards or vectors, regardless of what they are, exact a cost among the people. To influence or force a population to adopt certain mindsets and behaviors inevitably has

---

[75] De Mente, Boyé Lafayette. (2012). *Korean Mind: Understanding Contemporary Korean Culture*

142

negative unintended consequences, especially when they are taken to an extreme. Any time that a high price is paid, and other choices are available, people will consider alternatives.

From a high-level perspective, is it possible to consider the cost/benefit ratio of a certain practice? Do the benefits outweigh the negatives? Should a specific cultural practice continue? As you can imagine, for a people to thrive and survive, this evaluation becomes an important part of self-examination. This very question highlights a dilemma: For a given culture, who makes this decision? And once the decision is made, what can one do about it?

To use a fascinating example, let's use China's one child policy. As China's economic conditions improved in the 20th century, families could afford to have more children, and improvements in health care allowed people to live longer. In addition, there has been a long-standing cultural bias for larger families, partially to help ensure that parents are cared for in their old age and to ensure the continuation of the family lineage.

This was perceived as a major problem by the Chinese government. The increased population was a barrier to the vision of the leaders for progress and the associated planned economy. Hence, the imposition of the groundbreaking one-child policy. In this modern era, this policy was considered quite unusual, wouldn't you agree?

- Imposing such a rule at the family level was very personal.
- Few other governments would be able to successfully implement this mandate.

History has shown that the one-child policy was very successful in slowing the population growth, but not surprisingly, it had unintended consequences. Here's one of them. Families tended to prefer sons over daughters. As the resulting demographics illustrate, families managed to give birth to many more sons than daughters, creating a gender imbalance.

Ironically, now that the leaders of China see the need to increase the population and balance out the ratio of older to younger citizens, a bottoms-up shift has happened. Many families have become accustomed to investing their resources and energy to provide solely for one child. They see having a second child as too expensive. When China rescinded the one-child policy, there was an initial bump in births, but many families are voluntarily limiting their family to one child, acting to address their own needs and desires.

What's my point? Whether it is a higher-level authority or a groundswell of public opinion, cultural behavior and its outcomes are consciously or subconsciously assessed for value. Adjustments are made, even within the course of a few years. The big difference is that today, people have unprecedented access to information and alternatives, and governments are finding it more difficult to control behavior. As people more clearly see the reality and fact-based outcomes of cultural standards, they tend to make personally driven decisions to better their own condition, rather than blindly conform. This is especially true when they have personal contact with others who are succeeding with non-conforming behavior. During the first years of COVID, I exchanged experiences with my friends in China, who were subject to a much tighter virus control plan. Even though one of my messages was censored due to my unintentional use of a banned tag, we were able to provide each other with helpful advice.

Simply put, when people have access to information, outcomes, and options, they will do what is best for their situation, defeating cultural norms. Having examined Korea in various ways, let's see how that experience jibes with some of the concepts we've shared.

1. The Net Effect — The ability of online interaction to build and alter cultures in ways that previously never existed.

Consider the stark difference between North and South Korea in terms of Internet access. In North Korea, extremely few people have any online access, and then only when it is in the interest of the state. The everyday person has no concept of the Internet and its expansive universe of information. The majority of North Koreans continue to believe that their country is the most powerful and richest in the world. I can't imagine that belief prevailing if online interaction with others were possible.

Early on in South Korea, the government supported an infrastructure of high-speed access. South Koreans are sophisticated online users and are heavy users of social media with the popular Line and Kakao apps. Likewise in culture, North Korea is frozen in time and South Korea moves on.

144

2. The Liquified Life — The potential for living a super-informed life that can easily flow and flex based on new and wide-ranging inputs.

Korea and Japan have many similarities. They both tend to see themselves as distinct from the rest of the world. They desire to preserve their uniqueness. Yet South Koreans are different in that they are often more willing and interested in accepting new inputs, learning from others. Many Japanese would rather keep outside influence at bay. Consider this. When Japanese students travel to the U.S. for university and come back to Japan to live and work, they are seen by some as tainted by foreign influence. A South Korean student, upon returning home, would be expected to take gained knowledge and apply it with his own native understanding to make Korea a better place.

North Koreans who have escaped the North need to adjust to South Korean independence. They are offered schooling to help them transition to a life where they are expected to make decisions, something the state has always done for them. In the book *In Order to Live: A North Korean Girl's Journey to Freedom,* Yeonmi Park relates how she was asked to introduce herself in such a school and share some of her interests. One of the questions was about her favorite color. The question confused her, and she couldn't answer. She assumed that there must be a correct answer, one that they wanted her to say, but she didn't know what that was.[76]

The point here is simple. There is a spectrum of openness. For a variety of reasons, people vary in their willingness and capability to take in and use external information. My bias is toward more openness.

3. Cultural Mind-map – The tendency for humans to conceptualize groups and to use these groups to make sense of themselves and others, despite the many contradictions.

How about this math question? If there are three American bastards and two of them die at the hands of our glorious leader, how many are left? Yes, this is a typical math lesson in North Korea. From what I have read, no one says "American" there without adding "bastard."

---

[76] Park, Yeonmi. (2015). *In Order to Live: A North Korean Girl's Journey to Freedom*

The South also conceptualizes people in North Korea in unflattering ways. I know of one South Korean adult who admits that as a child he was looking for horns on the heads of North Koreans the first time he saw them on TV. Because devils have horns.

People are trying to make sense of the Korean border, this division of a people once united. If there is conflict and we are the good guys, well, the other guys must be the enemy.

4. Cultural Vectors — Actively supported, positive ideals embedded within a culture that are considered the more, the better.

North Korea has a cultural vector that promotes devoted service to a "god," their supreme Leader. How about the work-hard vector? A few years ago, I hiked up a small mountain outside of Seoul guided by a 30-something South Korean woman. When I asked her if Koreans work hard and show little emotion, her response was, "Yes, and that is why we are so unhappy." From what we see, the new generation of South Koreans might not conform to such extreme expectations.

In summary, I hope that I have pointed out some characteristics of Korea that contribute to an understanding of the overall human condition. I admire the Korean people. As we said earlier, they have demonstrated their strength and fortitude through many challenging times. 작은 고추가 맵다. "A small pepper is hot."

Top-Down Culture

Kings, emperors, presidents — they demand attention. They are an influential part of the environment that shapes culture and our boundaries. In our world, top-down cultures are being defined and manipulated by leaders. Tying our personal pathways too closely to fallible leaders can put us on a course that does not align with our true selves and our personal needs. Political leaders have their own agendas, and they tend to live in a very isolated environment.

Two Kings of Thailand

In October 2016, the reigning king of Thailand, King Bhumibol Adulyade, died. He was 88 and had ruled Thailand for 70 years. His death was a shock. For most people, he was the only king they had known. Many were crushed. The government asked people to limit any entertainment for a month and to dress in a way to reflect mourning for one year. All civil servants were asked to wear black for a year as a sign of mourning. How's that for a cultural expectation?

The king was revered by many. He was considered an advocate for the people, community, and tradition. Words of praise came from around the world, from Putin to Obama to UN Secretary-General Ban Ki-moon. He had ruled through more than a dozen military coups and 20 prime ministers.

While he seemed to engender genuine praise and respect, he also had the law on his side. In Thailand, to criticize the king or anyone connected to him is against the law and could land someone in jail for up to 15 years. How's that for a strong motivation?

Which brings us to the reign of the new king, his son. King Maha Vajiralongkorn is approaching his position in a new way. Even before his coronation, he took personal control of the Crown Property Bureau, which handles over $30 billion in assets. Later, he signed a new military-backed constitution, blocked his sister from running for prime minister, and took over two army units.

Then he got tongues wagging by bestowing the title of "royal noble consort" to a young woman, something that had not been done since polygamy was outlawed in 1935. A consort functions as a companion and partner to the king. The arrangement didn't last long. A few months after the bestowing, the king stripped the consort of all her titles. She was called "disloyal," "ungrateful" and "ambitious." Shortly thereafter, it was announced that six senior palace officials were dismissed for "extremely evil" conduct.

How quickly things change. The new king seems uninterested in maintaining the existing cultural norms or transitioning to a new culture. Apparently, he'd rather expand his power base and address his personal preferences. As a leader for life, the king doesn't have to worry about getting re-elected, but the court of public opinion has a lot of influence in the 21st century. It's too early to say if the king is simply interested in expanding his power to insulate himself and support his lifestyle or if he intends to shift the cultural framework of the country. My guess is that any new cultural framework will have to be formed by someone else or by way of a bottoms-up initiative of the people. My bet is that many Thai people will simply look fondly to the past rule of the former king and proceed to follow their own individual paths, behavior that the new king has already modeled.

The new Thai king is not alone in moving away from a traditional royal lifestyle. In the United Kingdom, Prince Harry and his wife recently announced that they were moving away from their royal roles, protocol, and obligations, apparently without Queen Elizabeth's blessing. This news was met with a mixed reaction, of course, but I suspect many are thinking, "Good for them. It's their life."

The result in Thailand is moving a step away from a cultural understanding between a king and his people that lasted 70 years and a step toward separate lives with limited cultural connections. Perhaps in those months of mourning, the people realized this new condition would become their future.

K-Pop to the Rescue

Prior to the Asian financial crisis in 1997, South Korea had been experiencing a tremendous economic boom. Their per capita GDP had risen from $324 in 1972 to $13,403 in 1996.[77] With the Asian financial crisis, the country found itself deep in debt. In December 1997, they managed to negotiate a $57 billion loan from the International Monetary Fund. The day of the loan request became known in Korea as the Day of National Humility.

Desperate to recover, Korea assessed its options. The direction they took was a surprising one. Lacking many natural resources and arable land, they turned to entertainment as a moneymaking strategy. The government established the Ministry of Culture. One of the goals of the new division was to promote the research and development of highly advanced "cultural technology." Here was a country steeped in years of culture reinventing itself with holograms and artificial rainbows.[78]

Korean drama, K-Pop, and Korean movies are now in high demand inside and outside of Korea. Success in the music industry was particularly unexpected as the government banned popular music in the 1970s. A risky five-year plan for the arts that started in 1972 eventually blossomed with success in the movie industry late in the 1990s. A healthy percentage of Korean films that were screened at the newly formed Busan International Film festival in Korea started being accepted in Cannes. In 2020, the Korean movie *Parasite* won four Academy Awards in the U.S. including Best Picture.

---

[77] Macrotrends https://www.macrotrends.net/countries/KOR/south-korea/gdp-per-capita
[78] Hong, Euny. (2014). *The Birth of Korean Cool.* p.99-100

The government of Korea, in partnership with private investment, manufactured a new outward culture for Korea, and it worked; it made money, lots of money. It didn't seem to matter to foreign consumers that the new cool culture wasn't consistent with the years of hardship and restraint that had previously characterized Korea. This was a new image that was open to elements of global culture mixed in with some universal themes of the Korean experience.[79] The government wasn't done. Shortly after Korean President Park Geun-hye took office in 2013, she established the Ministry of Future Creation and Science for the next generation of the creative economy, with a mixed reaction. The backlash that President Park took for this new initiative was on multiple fronts — one regarding concern for the budget and the other regarding anxiety over the divergent cultural direction.

Divine Rule in Japan

I suggest that we look at another extreme case, that of the royal family of Japan. It's a story of service, love, and rigid tradition. The country of Japan, as you probably know, tends to hold tight to their cultural practices. While Korea aspires to be an island, Japan truly is.

For perspective, let's travel back in time a bit. You might have heard of Emperor Hirohito, the emperor and supreme commander of Japan during World War II. The extent of his involvement in Japan's aggression is still under debate. Regardless, he had a lot of influence. Back then, the emperor was generally considered a divine figure, something the Buddhist and Shinto sects supported. Students were taught that the Japanese race and nation were chosen and set apart from others. They had their own version of manifest destiny called Kudo, which played into the idea of expanding Japan's rule. Divine rule and a cultural belief in imperialist expansion helped push the Japanese into war.

The office of the emperor was so important that when it was evident that Japan was going to lose the war, the leaders held out, afraid that surrender would mean the end of the reign of emperors. Hirohito himself held on until the second atomic bomb was dropped on Nagasaki and the Soviets invaded Japanese territory. At that time, he announced the surrender (without using the word) to the Japanese people in an historic

---

[79] Snyder, S. A. (2021) The two Koreas. *Foreign Policy Association* p72-3

radio broadcast. The powerful, formal, and eloquent voice of the emperor was thought to be a critical factor in ending the war. Despite the defeat, the office of the emperor was permitted to live on, partly due to the thinking that a cooperative emperor would help a great deal in the country's postwar transformation.

In summary then, during the early 1940's, the emperor of Japan was able to:

- Lead the country into war as a divine figure.
- Delay the end of war.
- End the fighting in a way no one else could do.

A brief comparison to the emperor of today will provide a stark contrast, showing how the cultural importance of the office has been diminished to a figurehead, leaving a heavy burden of rituals to the royal couple. What the war didn't destroy, the modern era has disparaged.

Much has changed from the time of Hirohito. The reverence and the relevance of the emperor's role has faded. Yet the strict adherence to rules and respect is still expected by some. In 1990, a photographer was banned for taking a picture of Emperor Akihito's bride brushing her hair out of her eyes. In 2001, the emperor was criticized for bringing up a distant Korean ancestor at a news conference, considered a misstep in a land where Japanese racial purity is highly valued.

In April 2019, the reigning Emperor Akihito announced to his son, Shinto priests, and chamberlains his abdication due to age and infirmity. This was an unusual departure from the practice of service until death. His successor, Emperor Naruhito, quickly felt the sting of lingering expectations. He was criticized when his wife spoke longer than him at their first news conference and walked a step ahead of him in public.

A strong cultural bond is required to instill and preserve a belief that a leader is a divine figure, someone who can do no wrong. Over the course of 75 years since the end of World War II, the office of the emperor lost this distinction.

It's another testimony to the factors we've discussed. The transparency of the Information Age has contributed to a shift in attitudes toward divinity and leadership in general. Highly visible human limitations have eroded the credibility of once dominant positions.

151

Japan itself is in a difficult place with its demographics. The Japanese have begun a slide toward negative population growth. Even though they can be very welcoming and gracious to visitors, the country in general is not receptive to immigrants or to intermarriage. While many admire the ability of the Japanese to retain much of their culture, the isolation and inflexibility are leading to contraction.

The small town of Nagoro, Japan, no longer has any children. The school was closed after the last student graduated. Low birthrates and lack of opportunity have led to this situation, which is common for many rural areas of Japan. What is uncommon is Nagoro's response. The small town was repopulated with lifelike dolls set up in poses and doing various activities. Over 300 dolls now grace the town, and it has become a tourist attraction.

United States Divided

The U.S. president wants to isolate the U.S. from other countries in the world. I feel like we are going to the past instead of the future. Separation between people is not good. (Venezuelan voice, Sunny)

There is no escaping a discussion of the United States and the phenomenon of the Trump presidency. We are not alone in trying to determine the meaning and consequence of this unusual, norm-breaking period. Emotions run high on all sides of this situation. This is a revealing piece of history, full of evidence of how people think and react.

The well-documented life of Donald Trump doesn't seem to me to model any culture. He is overwhelmingly concerned with two things, his public image and wealth. He does speak about cultural values that resonate with many people. The primary message, the one that seems to afford him the most support, is a special brand of patriotism. Here's the formula: What is good for America is good for you, and I am good for America. It's a clear message and it has worked well for him. He has hijacked patriotism and transformed his message into a cultural vector. Trump is making the case, the more of me, the better. There is an emotional component here that tends to bind people to the message and the person delivering it.

For many, he has become something of a cult figure. As you know, a cult figure is someone who evokes an emotional and psychological bond that allows him to become larger than life and deflect criticism. How else could someone who has divorced multiple times, rarely goes to church, and seems to lack a basic understanding of Christianity become a hero for the religious right? Despite over 16,000 documented lies over the course of his presidency, his base supporters remain extremely loyal.

As a president, the level of daily personal, very public communication is unprecedented. He has tweeted over 10,000 times. The language is very basic and unpresidential. His opinions are extreme. There are the very bad guys and the very good guys, nothing in between. He is speaking to his base and telling them what they want to hear. He signs Bibles, which would seem totally inappropriate; but because he is serving as their cultural icon, his actions have become the new standard.

Let's get back to how this relates to our theories on culture. I believe that the intensity of support for Trump comes from the reality that many of the cultural values he promotes are dying, and people know it. They long for the days, now past, where most people share the same values and culture. They now live in a world where people from many different places live together. Their own historically dominant culture is melting away.

Just listen to someone who grew up on a dairy farm in New England and later went to a seminary to help her small town. She shares what seems to be a common sentiment, saying, "Our culture continues to decline, our families continue to fall apart, our schools continually do worse and worse." She adds, "I haven't been able to drain the swamp. The alligators are everywhere."[80]

We can see how people have different reactions to personal challenges that are due to environmental changes. People can respond defensively and resist, or they can analyze and adapt. This begs the question, what factors determine which direction people will take?

Logically, the size of the change would be a factor. If the change challenges core fundamental values of the group, resistance would be more likely. The other key factor might be resource availability. If the person has information, alternatives, and the means to adjust, adaptation

---

[80] Wuthnow, Robert. (2018). *The Left Behind: Decline and Rage in Rural America*

becomes more practical. Either way, a charismatic leader could influence people in a certain direction.

The biggest threat to humanity is that without a shared understanding of how to live their life under current conditions, people will blindly follow the dictates of a galvanizing and dictatorial voice. That voice will find some class of people to blame for the world's problems. Look no further than the lies that were spread to fuel the angry and misguided challenge to the presidential election in 2020. That environment paves the way for authoritarian rule.

Hong Kong's Cultural Crossroad

Would it be possible for me to discuss Hong Kong without getting mired down in geopolitics? Hong Kong is going through a difficult transition. Yes, the UK and China have agreed on a 50-year buffer between British rule and full China integration. For now, it is "one China, two systems." But what Hong Kong will be like in 2047 is still unknown, and that tends to breed fear for those involved.

Hong Kong is faced with a sandwich generation. Older parents in Hong Kong seem less concerned about the future state of Hong Kong and are less critical of mainland China influence. Young adults, born around the time of the 1997 agreement, see themselves losing autonomy. Yet another generation, the young Hong Kong children of today, are being taught Mandarin Chinese, the language of the mainland, and are being assimilated into the coming world. They, like their grandparents, might see the cultural and societal convergence as inevitable and acceptable.

Is that all it takes for a significant cultural transformation in this new era of mass communication? Two generations? Hong Kong is not usual in this regard. But will this shift from the culture of the past be toward a new society, largely without an identifiable, grass-roots culture?

Mao and the Cultural Revolution

"Great and earthshaking historical changes have taken place in China in the 20th century." — From the preamble to the Constitution of the People's Republic of China.

To truly appreciate what has happened in China over the last 100 years or so, one must understand some history. While there are very few written records of the time, the first dynasty, Shang, is said to have begun around 1600 BC. Imperial dynasties as a form of rule in China existed (with some gaps) until 1911, when the Qing dynasty ended with the Xinhai Revolution. That's remarkable — a single form of government for about 3,500 years!

Since then, China experienced a great deal of transformation while struggling to redefine itself as a country and as a government. From 1912 to 1949, the Republic of China existed. It endured while China suffered and fought through World War II.

After the war, the conflict between the ruling Kuomintang and the Communist Party led by Mao Zedong intensified and was eventually won by the communists. As a result, the People's Republic of China was established in 1949.

To summarize Chinese history: Imperial dynasties lasted 3,500 years. The Republic of China lasted 38 years. In 2019, the People's Republic of China celebrated 70 years.

Someone need only consider the practice of binding feet in China to illustrate the extent of recent changes. Foot binding started a thousand years ago when the emperor's favorite concubine danced for him on feet that were bound into a hoof-like shape. Realizing how the emperor was pleased, the other concubines attempted to copy the foot-binding practice and the fashion spread throughout China. By the mid-17th century, every woman who intended to marry would have her feet bound.

The binding of feet was extremely painful and was initiated when the girls were between 4 and 6. It involved bending the toes of the girls until they were under their soles and holding them there with ribbons. Whenever the feet grew too large, it was necessary to break the feet to keep them in place. As you can imagine, walking on these bound feet was difficult and tiring and required a special technique.

Binding feet was at the height of its popularity in the 19th century. As you might expect, foot binding was eliminated because of the increased interaction with other cultures. Missionaries came from the Western countries to China and discouraged the practice. The abolishing of foot binding was also supported by educated Chinese who came back from studies abroad in Europe. You might be surprised to hear that the practice continued until the time of the fall of the Qing dynasty in 1911-12.

For now, we are going to focus on the Cultural Revolution (1966-1976), an important part of the early years of the People's Republic. I can't imagine a richer environment for gleaning cultural insights. The Mao Zedong era lasted the first 28 years of the Republic of China. During that time, Mao assumed different leadership roles and initiated many different programs designed to move China ahead. The Great Cultural Revolution was one of them.

Prior to the Cultural Revolution, Mao had initiated the Great Leap Forward, which had some serious problems. Mao wanted to transform the agricultural economy to an industrial one leveraging the large labor pool in China and the collectivization of farms. He set some very aggressive goals.

To help reach these goals, Mao suggested that people could take their metal tools and melt them down using makeshift backyard steel furnaces to be set up in every village. Unfortunately, the steel produced by this process was generally of low quality and the resulting lack of metal tools stymied other progress.

This is one example of the limitations of the Great Leap Forward. When village leaders were afraid to report poor results and problems, the planning process was unable to course correct. The result was the starvation of many millions of people.

What was Mao to do? He began his rule with a tremendous amount of public support. As a general, he had led the communist forces which beat the Kuomintang and then redistributed the wealth of the Kuomintang landowners. But with the failure of the Great Leap Forward, he distanced himself from the people for a time. Before long, he had his new idea. Mao set upon his new initiative, that of the Great Cultural Revolution. Here was a man who understood the power of culture.

Mao seemed at his best when he took the position of the people's leader. He did not adopt the language and tradition of the emperors. He spoke simply. His most effective proclamation of the need for a cultural revolution was to write a big character poster, a communication technique used by the common people. It was a call to action, to "Bombard the Headquarters." It spoke of misguided "leading comrades" who were "suppressing revolutionaries." He further established himself as the people's leader when he showed up at an event to swim in the dirty Yangtze River with several thousand other people. Imagine a 72-year-old leader in his swimming trunks waving to an adoring crowd after his swim. Honored by his presence among them and impressed by his energetic swim they shouted, "Long live Chairman Mao!"

The campaign of the revolution was not intended to return the country to the imperial past, but to destroy the "Four Olds" — old customs, old culture, old habits and old ideas. People were urged to embrace the wisdom of the Little Red Book, titled the *Quotations of Chairman Mao*, and to stay true to China's form of communism. People were expected to read, memorize and quote Mao's sayings.

People generally equate a revolution to a war. Many wars have been fought to topple corrupt governments. Here instead was a battle from within to gain the hearts of the people by applying social pressure to conform to the stated philosophical approach. Don't get me wrong, there was plenty of violence and conflict associated with China's purging of the old and instigating of the new, but it wasn't a military war. Many people who look back at the Mao era have different conclusions.

As we have seen time and again, humans, especially in times of stress and change in their environment, long for a set of guidelines and shared beliefs. Internalizing and acting on these shared beliefs can be emotionally rewarding. Whatever else you think about Mao's history, his Little Red Book encapsulated and communicated a culture to a people who were looking to understand the changed world around them.

Environmental conditions such as economic downturns are often seen as the cause of discontent in the general population. Another source of discontent is the lack of a usable cultural framework that gives comfort and direction to a people in times of change. Some countries react by attacking what they see as cultural enemies, proposing barriers, exiting agreements and regressing. Lacking a strong, up-to-date culture that encompasses the realities of the modern world, some people adopt outdated cultures of the past, go on defense, or blindly follow the strongest voice. Alternatively, there is value in confidently building your own pathway based on your own environment and needs, independent of the institutional voices.

North Korea, Iran, China, South Korea, and the U.S. span the spectrum of totalitarian to democratic rule, but they all depend on a psychologically stable population, something a healthy, grass-roots culture supports. Repressive rule on the one hand and affluent indifference on the other are not enough to ensure stability.

Chapter 11

Cultures need a Moral Compass
Swedish Voice

Here is someone with flexibility and openness that reminds me of the Liquified Life, yet he calls himself stubborn. Maybe that is his Swedish humility. His flexibility does have limits, and those limits center on moral principles.

Name: Lars

Self-description: Positive, stubborn person who always believes in people being good.
(Born and raised in Sweden, lived over three years in Belgium, in France, and now living in the U.S.)

Cultural Values

From the start of the 20th century until the late 1940s, the Swedish culture encouraged people to remain humble, dim themselves down and stay low-key. We have an ethical value that we are all born equal. It is a Protestant country with a Lutheran state church. Even though we tend to have Christian values, about the only native Swedes who go to church are the ones that work there.

Since the 1930s and 1940s, the strong welfare system created a culture and a message that the state will take care of you, which isn't necessarily true. Everyone receives free schooling and free health care and pays high taxes. People tend to have less motivation to do better than others.

Risk-taking in Sweden is pretty strong. We are entrepreneurial, partly because of the safety net of the state welfare system. Sweden is consistently in the top five or 10 countries for innovation.

Generational Changes

My parents were born before the baby boomers, in the '30s. In their lives, work comes before anything else. There is more life balance in my generation, and now millennials tend to work when they can fit it in. They are more risk takers, perhaps because the older generations can now fund them. More lifestyle choices exist today, which people can access through education or work.

The suppressed culture of the past is changing, and millennials don't live that way. This change is not so much a Swedish thing; it's more of a global thing.

Cultural Integration

For the last 40-50 years, even more so the last five to 10 years, Sweden has seen quite heavy immigration. Swedish culture is now getting more blended with other cultures, which I believe is positive.

People raised in Sweden complain about how the immigrant population in Sweden lives separately in apartments with satellite dishes and in neighborhoods with specialized stores. They wonder why the immigrants don't integrate more. When I moved to Belgium as an ex-pat, I lived in a city south of Brussels that was about 25 percent ex-pats. We lived in apartments with satellite dishes and in neighborhoods with specialized stores. Just the same.

There is no such thing as a perfect integration; if I stay here in the U.S. the rest of my life, I would call this my home and Sweden my home. To integrate into Sweden, the most important thing is to learn the language, even if you know English well. Without knowing Swedish, you can't be fully integrated. In many immigrant or ex-pat families, the working parent has learned Swedish for work and the kids have learned Swedish in school, but the stay-at-home parent hasn't learned Swedish and is not well integrated. You can't force people to integrate; the people must want it.

More Swedes started going to the U.S. in the '80s. When I first went to the U.S. at age 12, there were no taco restaurants in Sweden. Today, tacos are one of the most popular foods in Sweden. Food is something that we get from other countries and want to experience in our own country.

In a more cosmopolitan setting, it is easier to work with other people because you are used to it. In Sweden, Syrian refugees are typically relocated into rural areas. When you have 500 immigrants in a small city of 4,000 with a strong culture, it will take a longer time for integration. I believe that cultural barriers can be bypassed by walking around them, climbing over them, or tearing them down. Generally, I don't believe in tearing cultural barriers down, I believe in working together. However, I would never accept a cultural trait that defends a practice that I would consider criminal or unfair to women, for example.

U.S. Cultural Differences

My biggest shock living here, and it bothers my kids as well, is to fill out a form and specify your ethnicity. In Sweden, you never ever check a box about your ethnicity.

I struggle with the segregation of the African American population in the U.S. I struggle with the problems of the indigenous population, which in many places of the world has a more difficult time. I struggle with the strong religious connections to business in the U.S., which we never see in Sweden.

Culture in the Future

I believe that extreme cultures (religious, political, etc.) might get impacted and become less extreme. More cultures will appear because of the mixes of cultures. There might also be a culture that is a complete blend of all cultures. That would still be a culture. I don't believe that you can live in a world where there isn't a culture, but the nature of culture, itself, might change.

I don't know who said it, but I strongly believe that "Culture eats strategy for breakfast." You can have all the good plans in the world, but if you don't account for the cultural piece, you are never going to succeed. If you think that one size fits all, you will have to rethink, because one size fits nobody.

My Observations and Reflections

Lars is a strong believer in the power of culture and in the goodness of people. His international experience informs his opinions. Cultures will always be there, he says, no matter what form they take. His idea of a mix of all cultures becoming a single separate culture is intriguing to me. That recipe would be a complicated one, but why not? Take all the best elements of each culture and create a new superior one. One problem: Cultures carry the sacredness of the collective experience of others. A piecemeal culture loses a connection to history.

No matter. The world is changing. What's worked in the past needs to be reconsidered. Not only do cultures need to keep up, but the way they are formed will likely change as well. It's important that we consider how to achieve the best results for everyone. A later chapter in this book is titled "Making our Way" for a reason. **Finding** our Way would imply that the right culture already exists for everyone and it's only a matter of finding it. **Creating** our Way would imply that we start from scratch and build it all ourselves. **Making** our Way is designed to acknowledge our current reality. We need to proactively decide as individuals and as a community how we use cultures and supplement them.

While Lars demonstrates a great deal of flexibility, he is disturbed by inequality. He struggles with unfair treatment of groups of people. If culture is changing, this is our opportunity to start moving in a better direction. Would it be possible to break free from our historical bias, preserve the good and jettison the bad? Lars sees the power of culture and values ethical principles. Can we have both?

Religion

Whatever the religion, each God (or enlightened one, such as Buddha) has made it a priority to give people a way of life and wisdom to guide them. Think the Bible, the Sutras, the Torah, the Book of Mormon and the Qur'an. It is not surprising to us that these supreme beings understand humanity's need to adopt a pattern of life and values.

"Foreigners should also know something about the principles and dictates of Islam, which is not merely a set of beliefs; rather, it dictates appropriate behavior patterns for every aspect of daily life." (Globesmart.com)

These directions range from the universal "love your neighbor as yourself" doctrine to very specific rituals. The way I see it, each god's love for people is manifested in the cultural guidance they provide them. For example, the Ten Commandments, the beatitudes, and the Shari'ah, the code for living for Muslims.

From my perspective, a couple of these cultural dimensions seem to be overlooked: forgiveness and redemption. In today's transparent world, sins of the people are becoming more visible and often lead to devastating social media commentary. As a result, a socially accepted process for forgiveness and redemption is even more important. Shouldn't there be a path back from social death? Ironically, despite the talk of forgiveness, we've seen how the religious community in practice can be especially harsh and demanding.

Religious cultures become dynamic as various prophets/holy people update and interpret them. There is some inherent danger to these addenda. If corrupt leaders or false prophets heap on all sorts of self-serving, misguided, or unnecessary rules, people might feel justified to opt out of a given spiritual culture.

"In vain do they worship me, teaching human precepts as doctrines." Mark 7:7, New Revised Standard Version (NRSV)

The opposite side of the spectrum can be damaging as well. If people hang on too long to traditions that are counter to prevailing values, conflict is likely.

Such is the ebb and flow of religious affiliation. Again, the transparency of the modern world and the expansion of choice disturb the status quo. In the modern world, people now learn about other religions in a variety of ways and are exposed to scandals and negative outcomes from religious leaders.

If cultures deserve principles that are respectful and just, can religion help? Religion and culture have a lot in common. Both have expectations that people share values and stay true to them.

I am Christian, ELCA Lutheran to be more specific. As a child, I was hungry for answers. When I was 10 years old, I found a guide at the back of my Bible for reading the Bible in a year. By reading two or three days' worth each day, I was able to read the entire Bible two times, cover to cover, within a year. Every two hours, I'd sit down and read the Bible and then recite to myself a long prayer that I had compiled. Through this experience I gained a sense of right and wrong that I believed at the time to be respectful and just. It had a profound effect on me, despite the many times I fell short. Lately, I have tried to simplify God's direction for me, using the words in Micah 6:8: "Do justice, love kindness, and walk humbly with God."

When my wife was a young girl, she would hold funerals for the neighborhood pets. Even though women were not allowed to be pastors at the time, she was determined to follow that path from an early age. She was ordained shortly after our daughter was born. As you can imagine, being the spouse of a pastor opened my eyes to many real-world problems and connected me to some inspiring people.

While I have faith in God, I also recognize the harm done by people in the name of Christianity. I also recognize my own shortcomings and mistakes and am grateful for the power of forgiveness. As I meet with people around the world, I try to be open and receptive, willing to learn from other religions and practices. It's a tremendous gift to understand what is important to others. On the other hand, I sometimes accuse myself of not being vocal enough about my own beliefs. Apparently, I have trouble walking the fine line of listening and sharing.

The Amish community and Rumspringa provide an interesting perspective on how we choose our religious direction. In many ways, they mirror current reality. The Amish communities belong to a traditionalist Christian church group. They live and dress simply and reject the use of modern technology. The Amish youth, sometime in their adolescence, enter Rumspringa, which is translated as "running, jumping, or hopping around." For each person, this special period might mean joining a youth group for social interaction or, at another extreme, partying and the use of unsanctioned technology. Amish youth are free to spend this time in self-reflection and to engage in exploration. Ultimately, after a few years, an Amish youth must decide whether to commit to the community and its way of life through baptism and marriage or to leave the community forever.

The theory is that by giving these youth the chance to explore activities outside of the community they know, they will be better equipped to make an informed decision on whether to commit. And because it will be their decision, they will be more likely to keep their commitment.

Think of the correlation to what we have discussed. In this example, there exists isolation in a tightly knit community, a well-defined way-of-life, and a period of choice. Youth are deciding between an established culture and the unknown. You might be surprised that studies show a large majority of teens elect to stay in the restrictive Amish community rather than move on to another lifestyle.

In analyzing the situation, one must consider that relatively few people in the U.S. experience a tightly knit community that provides many cultural guidelines. The Amish experience demonstrates the value of a community culture in a world of choice. To someone from that tight community, the external world might seem filled with distractions and devoid of meaning.

Religion, then, has a close relationship to culture. Like culture, a religion must remain relevant over the years to new environments. What's more, many religions seem to be facing the same challenges as cultures, losing their guiding hand on people's lives.

In an article titled "How Should We Think About Declining Denominational Numbers" in *Christianity Today* by John Davidson, culture is identified as a factor in church involvement. "The church doesn't exist in a vacuum. It's inextricably tied to culture and context. So, whatever is happening in culture will impact the church. It always has."[81]

Regarding culture, there is a lot to learn from what religion is experiencing today.

- Both culture and religion rely on shared experiences and beliefs. Both rely on a spiritual dimension that animates thought, feeling, and action.
- Religions promote the creation of a supportive cultural foundation through their teachings.
- An environment that fails to sustain a culture will likely fail to sustain a religion as well.

---

[81] Davidson, John. (2019, June 18). How Should We Think About Declining Denominational Numbers? *Christianity Today*

Racism and Sexism

In my country we only have white people. Russians still watch international people like they are from another planet. They watch every piece of their body. It is not that they don't trust them, but they are curious. They watch to understand and accept a different culture. (Russian voice, Есения)

*I work with people from many different countries. I always have the pressure of different cultures. Like the Indian people, we do support for them. It's a little bit difficult to deal with them, because of the way they handle the work. Another example is when we work with the Japan team. They are polite, but they are not very straightforward. The people from Latin America seem to be very happy. (*Chinese voice, 颖怡)

Ninety-nine percent of the people know that we are the same. Treating others like you'd like to be treated. We are all the same. We all know each other, but somehow that darkness, something in the back of our head, says that they are different. (Hmong voice, Fwmtxaam)

Racism

There is a close relationship between race and culture. In history, as people of a particular race moved (or were moved) from one place to another, they took their established culture with them, as well as their distinctive physical characteristics. When those physical characteristics distinguished them as "foreigners" and they were collectively ostracized, they continued to have a shared experience based on new perceptions, challenges and resistance. Often, this served to prolong differences and create a newly adapted, shared culture. Race and culture are two different things, but they are often linked.

Cultural and racial differences intersect in mixed marriages. A study of data from 1990 to 2001 in the *Survey of Income and Program Participation* (SIPP) suggests that overall, interracial marriages are less stable than same race/ethnicity marriages. But the data also supported the conclusion that marital dissolution is strongly associated with the specific races or ethnicity of the individuals in the union.[82] In fact, at least one type of interracial marriages (involving Asians and whites) was more stable than same-race white marriages. Mixed marriages involving blacks and whites were the least stable followed by Hispanic-white couples. I am guessing that cultural compatibility has something to do with that.

Expectations for the use of language have risen regarding racism. Certain words are taboo. Words used in communications are scrutinized for bias and insensitivity with real social consequences for failure to meet various and sometimes shifting standards. There seem to be multiple motivations. One is to elevate the dialog so that healthy attitudes around race and gender are reinforced both for the communicator and the receivers. In so doing, hurtful and damaging situations are avoided. Another motivation seems to be calling out people who don't meet the standard.

These dilemmas within cultures are not new. The complication we face today is that there are so many competing voices that are exposed in our

---

[82] Zhang, Y. & J. Van Hook. (2009). "Marital Dissolution Among Interracial Couples," *Journal of Marriage and Family*, vol. 71, no. 1.

connected world. Who gets to set the rules and who enforces them? Is there a process for reconciliation? Is racism a behavior we can influence or an immutable state of mind?

In a prior chapter, we covered how humans love to categorize things, and race is one way to categorize people. To explore this further, let me introduce an exercise. Please fill in the blanks as suggested below.

_____ people are _____ .

For the first blank, please use Asian, Black, Indian, White or other similar possibilities.

In the second blank, use lazy, crazy, hard-working, smart, self-centered or whatever you'd prefer.

Now please answer this question. Would the sentence be racist with any combination of the words given? It would seem so based on the dictionary definition. From dictionary.com: "Racism is a belief or doctrine that inherent differences among the various human racial groups determine cultural or individual achievement."

Basically, racism is distinguishing one race from another through the attribution of positive or negative characteristics. Now compare the following statements:

- Based on extensive research, we have found that people of American Indian heritage tend to form closer knit communities than our control group.
- As a member of the Caucasian race, I find that we are much more arrogant than others.
- Asian people are smarter and more hardworking than all other races.
- The French are suspicious of early friendliness in the discussion and dislike first names, removal of jackets, and the disclosure of personal or family details. [83]

All statements appear to be racist according to our definition. Which one is the most racist?

---

[83] This assertion is listed in a book my former boss gave me to help me deal with the cultures I was facing. Lewis, Richard D. *When Cultures Collide: Leading across Cultures*. USA: Nicholas Brealey Publishing, 2006

- **Statement number one:** The conclusion is based on a study. The observation is tempered by using "tend to." Also, the "closer-knit" attribute would generally be considered a positive one.

- **Statement number two:** The person is talking about his own race and the observation is self-deprecating.

- **Statement number three:** We don't know the race of the speaker, but the attribute is a positive one, and it's a view that I have heard others express.

- **Statement number four:** This is a list of generalized behaviors, asserting a pattern of suspicions and dislikes.

Are all these statements bad? Wrong? Are they less wrong if they are consistent with your experience, are based on a formal study, or if the attribute is a compliment? Are they more wrong if they are used to make an important decision? Are they OK if they are used to right a wrong? My Chinese American friend, a victim of racism herself, told me that the important distinction is intent. If people are using a statement to harm others, it is racism.

Race has been a way to separate people into different classes and justify different treatment, often cruel and dehumanizing. Racism distorts the essence of people. There are those among the powerful who understand the tendencies of people to classify and categorize others. Some use this tendency to their advantage. They propagate falsehoods about groups of people to maintain the status quo. We have seen how racism can be deeply imbedded into a culture. As racism gets built into a society, established systems perpetuate it. Most people now realize how ridiculous and horrible that tendency is.

Cultures are amazing manifestations of collective human behavior and beliefs. Cultures, like the people that form them, deserve respect and appreciation. Cultures also need moral oversight, a moral compass to guide them. When a culture harbors racism due to ignorance or greed, that racism must be purged.

I am confused about the desired goals in relation to race and culture. Could the assimilation of one culture into another ever be a good thing? How about if they combine in a way where both cultures impact each other? Or is it better to maintain a pure set of separate cultures and prolong cultural practices for as long as possible? Can each person make their own decision?

Years ago, many people seemed to believe that by pretending to be colorblind, they could erase racial prejudice and stereotypes. That is, if people could ignore the color of others, everyone could live together peacefully and equally. That didn't seem to work so well. Humans have trouble turning off their tendency to classify and judge. Did people really think that plan would erase years of prejudice? Today, thinking has shifted. Now, we hear that people of different colors are so diverse that it is wrong to assume that someone of one color can legitimately understand or speak for the experience or feelings of the other.

On the other hand, people are people. We are very much the same biologically. Often, the perceptions and imposed experiences created by systemic racism are what separates us. As a white male, I acknowledge the privilege that I have received over my lifetime and the difficulty I have truly understanding the pain and barriers caused by racism and bias. For me, I hope that learning about the lives of others around the world has helped me gain some degree of understanding.

Over 150 types of unconscious bias have been documented. Confirmation bias, insider bias, attribution bias and overconfidence bias are some examples. Your unconscious mind is busy processing over 99% of your sensory input because your conscious mind can only handle so much at a time. Cultures help people determine which unconscious biases to ignore, minimize or emphasize, but they can't make them completely go away. As we move into a world without traditional cultures, people will be "on their own" to a greater degree. They might take in standards where they can find them, perhaps from government-fabricated cultures, social media influencers, or work cultures.

Unfortunately, to the degree that people see distinctions between races as having value for them, they will be tempted to manufacture these distinctions and use them. The perceived value might be psychological, as in "I am better because my race is better," or as a practical means to an end. Personal self-interest will not disappear. The connections in people's brains will continue to fire, consciously or unconsciously.

It is hard to imagine changing bias within world cultures when just addressing bias within a company culture has proven so difficult. From a broad study that conducted statistical analyses on 829 firms over 31 years, the three most popular diversity programs (diversity training, evaluations, and network programs) showed **no positive effect**. Less popular programs such as mentoring and diversity managers were among the most effective.[84]

The idea that fewer people will wholeheartedly embrace broad-based cultures leads us to a world where individuals have less guidance from pre-assembled patterns of behavior. Perhaps the conceptual framework whereby it is assumed that large groups of people share common characteristics will become outdated, just as many other notions of the past have become debunked superstitions. For example, consider the notion from the pseudoscience of phrenology that skull shape can predict personalities.

The current racial framework could be influenced by three major trends. Number one, the explosion of the availability of data will prove many of the conclusions about group characteristics are wrong. The explosion of information and access to it in the last 50 years has been amazing. Yes, people are capable of avoiding and denying the truth, and yes, information access is not yet reaching everyone, but I hope that it's only a matter of time before we reach the tipping point.

Number two, without the binding nature of broad-based cultures, people will continue to become more and more dissimilar, making assumptions even less accurate. Shared traditional cultures are a major reason why groups of people behave similarly. Without them, the reduced social pressure for conformity will mean more diversity. There is evidence that as people see variations between people in a different race, they are less likely to stereotype them.[85] Assigning attributes to groups will become more problematic and less rewarding.

Number three, assuming the quality of life will continue to increase around the world, the tactic of using hate to divide people for gain will be more difficult, resulting in fewer manufactured differences. The growth of prejudice can accelerate when a group of people are suffering, and it

---

[84] Dobbin, F., Kalev, A., & Kelly, E. (2007). Diversity management in corporate America

[85] Nordell, Jessica, *The End of Bias: A Beginning,* 2021, p.251-2

becomes expedient to blame another set of people. Favorable living conditions will work against that.

For me, the fastest and most enduring path to breaking down racial stereotypes is to get to know a diverse group of people well. This leads (again) to the Liquified Life. With an unrestrained flow of information, a flexible population whose basic needs are met, and open empathetic minds, those who are receptive to learning will flourish. An unrealistic dream?

Sexism

Many of the cultures in the world have stark differences in the roles for men and women as well as separate opportunities and rewards. Certainly, cultures have played a part in perpetuating this condition. Through time, cultural drivers led people to create complementary, specialized roles for men and women, perhaps for efficiencies, perhaps for more selfish reasons. In the process, identities were formed. The assignment of male and female characteristics became a part of the social fabric, which reinforced the separate roles. Those who dared to challenge gender expectations faced strong pressure to conform. Generations grew up thinking these patterns were fixed. Religious teachings were used to lock in the cultural expectations.

To some people, the relationship of culture and gender has felt natural. Cultures tend to define roles for different categories of people. Women and men, with their different physical characteristics, are convenient categories, especially considering their distribution within families. With the animals around them, males and females often performed different roles, so our ancestors may have thought, why not humans?

The negative consequences of this arrangement have become obvious over time, just like they have in other situations where different groups of people are cast into narrowly defined roles. Inevitably, there is a power differential. Those with greater power continue to define roles to suit their needs and desires. Barriers are established to maintain the status quo. Corrupted by entitlement and power, people in positions of control commit abuses.

Today, many people would like to undo the barriers and level the playing field for everyone. In a sure sign that the nature of culture is changing, the ideal of equality is beginning to override the strongly established gender-based cultural guidelines. Equality has often enjoyed support as a cultural value, but in some places, equality is breaking away from its dependence on culture to become a universal value.

What's the difference between my notion of a cultural value and a universal value? Cultural values (what I've called cultural vectors) are strongly supported within the group, but the values are bounded by practical needs within a holistic, operational culture. As an example, self-sufficiency could be a cultural value, but a culture will limit its application because of other cultural demands. Self-sufficiency is only part of the cultural bundle. In times of crisis such as illness, requests for help might indeed be supported within the culture and supersede the value of self-sufficiency.

In contrast, the independence and power of a universal value tend to prevail regardless of history, stereotypes and other barriers. It will transcend a variety of cultures. In the interview with Lars from Sweden, you heard how he's navigated through his many cultural interactions with sensitivity, and yet he won't tolerate any cultural trait that defends a practice he considers unfair to women. In his case, equality overrides conflicting gender-based norms.

Cultural values are the collective beliefs of a group of people who share similar experiences and goals. These values have been formed, shaped, and hardened because they fill the very human needs of these groups. The issue is when a so-called universal value (such as gender equality) is positioned to negate long standing cultural values because the existing values have been deemed morally wrong. There is no easy solution. Lars has concluded that culture will eat strategy for breakfast. In other words, cultural values will prevail even when an external entity tries to make them obsolete.

This is the balancing act. All people deserve respect, respect for who they are and what they believe. I agree with Lars that we must choose to set limits on what we will tolerate. That doesn't mean that the universal notion of equality is easy to define or implement. Which of the following is most equal in terms of public restrooms?

- One restroom for all.
- Women's and men's restrooms, both with the same number of stations and similar facilities, both painted yellow.

- Women's and men's restrooms, with more stations in the women's due to the greater demand and longer wait times.
- Standard women's and men's restrooms supplemented by individual private restrooms for non-binary customers.

How about the soccer controversy? The U.S. women's soccer team, winner of four World Cups and four Olympic gold medals, has been very vocal in demanding pay and other benefits equal to those received by member of the U.S. men's team, which failed to qualify for the 2018 World Cup. In a lawsuit against the U.S. Soccer Federation, the federation defended its policy by claiming that the job performed by players on the women's team requires less skill, effort and responsibility than that required of the men. They argued that laws governing equal pay apply to jobs that require equal skills.

That logic applied was met with plenty of resistance in the court of public opinion. Shortly after the court filing became public, the president of the U.S. Soccer Federation resigned. Ultimately, with an agreement in 2022, the pay between the two teams was equalized, at least for now.

Who's right? On the one hand, the success and likability of the women's team has been a factor driving this lawsuit forward. Popularity and social media influence are real forces, but can they be legal arguments? On the other side, the demand for conformity to cultural ideals of male and female roles also has no legal standing.

Who's winning? The universal value of equality is gaining ground, and rigid cultural gender-based roles are losing. But there's a long way to go.

Chapter 12

Families are the Lifeblood of Culture
Laotian and Hmong Voices

Laotian Voice

In the following interview, we hear about multiple cultural conflicts. It is not easy to be Laotian, married to a Hmong man and living in the U.S. But I don't see her giving up.

Name: Keo (Angelica)
Self-description: Strong Woman, mother, wife

(Laotian, born in Laos, living in the U.S.)

I lived in Laos until 8 years old, then a refugee camp in Thailand for six months. Moved to U.S. in 1979 with stays in multiple cities.

Digital Influence
The people that I communicate digitally with are all in the U.S., but 90% were born in a different country.

Facebook is a cover-up, people don't share negative stuff, I don't believe everything that I hear on Facebook. To learn about someone, who they are, requires meeting in person. Facebook shares too much. Repeating of negative news, such as cop shooting. It is extremely overwhelming.

Language
In the early '80s, language was a big barrier for me. You need to know the language first. Independence requires learning to speak the language, to be able to read and write. That allows one to function without having to conform. I am constantly reminded of the importance of language when I care for my mom, who doesn't speak English well.

I never felt like I need to change myself to get along with others. Once I learned the language, I could understand better, but I didn't need to change.

Cultural Expectations
My family, culture is everything to us. Depends on the family. I understand how culture can be lost. Some families emphasized English rather than Lao language, but many realized that they were losing something.

Fact that I married a Hmong person rather than Laotian has resulted in struggles because of the resistance from other people. I will never be "Hmong enough" for my husband's family. In our culture, the mother-in-law owns the daughter-in-law, even more than her own daughter. As daughter-in-law, you are expected to get up early and have breakfast prepared for your mother-in-law before she wakes up.

Even now, if a traditional Hmong man wants to marry my daughter, I will expect a dowry to show respect. The money is not to buy, but to show respect for the people involved.

Hmong Voice

Here's the husband of the Laotian woman that we just heard from. He has some interesting philosophical ideas. Do you agree with him that everyone is the same?

Name: Fwmtxaam (Chan)
Self-description: Family man, friend, community member
(Hmong, born in Laos, lived in a Thai refugee camp after leaving
Laos, currently living in U.S.)

Cultural Interaction

I don't have any problem with any culture. Always a curiosity to know more. The more you know about other people, the more you learn about yourself. After a certain amount of questions, you find things you have in common.

Language can be a barrier. People speak different kinds of English language. Different terms and ways of speaking. Even after 30, 40 years you can have misunderstandings.

For one thing, being an Asian American, you look at your image first before adapting into an environment, to be accepted. Automatic thing you think about when you are a minority, never goes away. Sometimes you don't speak up, turn down opportunities. Because it isn't worth the fight. Sometimes being happy within yourself is better than a daily struggle.

In my culture, there is a lot of respect for your elders and ancestors, no matter what. By doing that, you respect them by doing what they expect. This is the greatest Hmong culture thing, that you don't step beyond that line. Health, happiness, prosperity and live to 120 years old.

Culture in the Future

I know that everyone has similarities. I hope in the future that everyone will respect everyone's differences. We all want the same thing; we just do it differently. We want good things, afterlife. Animals are like us. Why can't we be like them in treating each other?

Ninety-nine percent of the people know that we are the same. Treating others like you'd like to be treated. We are all the same. We all know each other, but somehow that darkness, something in the back of our head, says that they are different, don't mess with them. Tells you that there is a line. But there isn't a line.

My Observations and Reflections

The Hmong and Laotian experiences are rich with examples of how cultures adapt. I've had the opportunity to experience and learn directly from these communities through funerals, graduations, and day-to-day life. I see the struggle to fit in and to keep traditions alive. It's an organic process with no one in total control of the group. When options become visible and viable, individuals can determine their own rules and destinations.

For Angelica, the family is all important. We've also heard from the other interviews how critical the family is for passing down a culture. It takes sacrifice. In the next chapter, you'll hear how each funeral within the Hmong culture lasts multiple days. Passing down a language is a years-long endeavor. Teaching spiritual beliefs that conflict with the prevailing culture demands persistence. Parents must decide which traditions, rituals, and beliefs are most relevant to the lives of their children. Flailing a load of rice and growing the opium poppy lost significance after the migration to the United States. Children often pay a price whenever they take a path outside the mainstream. We also know, regardless of the culture, the family unit is undergoing change and conflict.

While in Belize, Central America, searching for a place to eat dinner, I came across reviews for a small family-run Italian restaurant. There was a negative review from someone who was disappointed with the food. To them, it wasn't the Italian food they were expecting. The frustrated owner replied and instructed the diner on the different types of Italian food from the different regions. His food was authentic, he stated, much more so than the popular chain restaurants catering to the American palate. In his mind, he made a choice to stay true to his roots. Yet the public is free to assert their own preference. We had our own disappointment with the restaurant. We made the long walk from town to the restaurant only to find it closed for an Italian holiday. In making decisions about what practices to keep and what to leave behind, there is not a right or wrong, but there are implications.

Hmong Cultural Transformation

I appreciate how until now we keep our culture. It is important to keep your culture, to take some good from international, but keep celebrating your holidays, and eat the special foods. (Russian voice, Есения)

How does a people, transplanted again and again from its native land, survive? The impact of those travels and environments on the Hmong culture has provided me with some eye-opening insights. The path of the Hmong people now living in the U.S. was long and difficult.

While many in the U.S. associate the Hmong with the country of Laos, they originally lived in the mountainous regions of southern China. Chinese historical sources indicate they were in China since 2000 B.C. Their move from China to Laos was prompted by disagreements and persecution.

The Hmong in China faced economic hardship and persecution by the Qing Dynasty government. China increased taxation to help pay indemnities to the British after losing the first Opium War in 1842. The Hmong fought against China in a series of wars but were unsuccessful. Many Hmong found it difficult to maintain their ethnic identity and practices in what they considered a hostile environment. This led to a great migration, with many of them settling in the mountains of Laos. Here they found terrain that was familiar to their homeland, a land that others found unsuitable. Perhaps here they could find a peaceful coexistence?

I find it inspiring that many Hmong were willing to leave China to maintain their cohesiveness. [86] For those who left China, problems continued in Laos. Again, they suffered under a burdensome tax, this time by the French, who had claimed Laos. A series of wars resulted in the establishment of an autonomous Hmong district. Then, internal political factions spilt the Hmong. When the Vietnam War started, one leader aligned with the French and later with the United States. Still another leader favored independence and became one of the leaders of the Laos Communist forces.

Because the Hmong in Asia had learned to grow opium and other crops with slash-and-burn techniques, they became experienced movers within Laos, frequently heading out to find new fertile land and unspoiled surroundings. These moves were less disruptive because they all moved together as a clan and village. They agreed upon a time and place. At the designated time, they disassembled their split bamboo and wooden plank homes and reassembled them in the new designated spot for the transported village.

Around the Hmong people, the world continued to stir trouble. In the Vietnam War, the U.S. battled to preserve the non-communist regime in South Vietnam. As a result, many Hmong were recruited to fight the communist forces and were given support from the U.S. When the Laotian government was overthrown in 1975, the next mass migration began in earnest. Facing difficult conditions and the threat of death, about one third of the Laotian Hmong made the dangerous journey to Thailand, and most ended up in refugee camps there. At the end of 1975, the U.S. began resettling Hmong from Thailand. By the early 1980s, about 50,000 Hmong were living in the US.

For this group of Hmong, their journey over the last 200 years was from China, to Laos, to Thailand and then the U.S. This migration gives us an opportunity to investigate a unique migration and resettlement that has now spanned both non-digital and digital periods in U.S. history. Here

---

[86] Even though many Hmong left China, by far the largest population of Hmong remains there, from 2 to 3 million people.

we have a group of people with strong cultural traditions that has already faced a mass migration and significant trials. Given that most of the Hmong immigrants came to the U.S. in the same 10-year period, they were a somewhat cohesive group. Most were born in either Laos, Thailand or the U.S.

A good portion of the Hmong diaspora ended up settling in California or Minnesota. Given Minnesota's radically different climate, this might seem surprising. Sponsorship was the overriding factor. The Lutheran church, which has a large concentration of members in Minnesota, took on the sponsorship of many Hmong people from the refugee camps in Thailand.

This Lutheran population in Minnesota has an immigrant history, too. Following the Reformation in Europe, Scandinavian countries and Germany had a significant Lutheran population. When they migrated to the U.S., over 100 years ago, they sought a land like the one they left. The plains of Minnesota, with land suitable for farming, was a desirable destination.

Due to the Lutheran church decision to sponsor Hmong immigrants, many second- and third-generation Lutherans in Minnesota welcomed and sponsored a new migrant population from a land, language, and culture vastly different from their own.

We are talking about a resilient and resourceful Hmong population here, but for any immigrant population and culture, they face various stages of adaptation.

- Survival — gaining access to the essentials of food and housing.
- Acclimations — becoming accustomed to a new environment.
- Self-sufficiency — having confidence in one's own resources; being able to meet one's needs without external assistance.
- Assimilation — adapting or adjusting to the culture of a region.

Not surprisingly, in this new world, the ties of family and clan are precious. Marriages between clans will occasionally be negotiated through clan leaders. In the Hmong world, names are important. At large family gatherings, someone may walk up to another and challenge them, "Do you know my name?" A failure to know might be punished with a demand to take a drink.

Speaking of drinking, the art of making moonshine was widely practiced by the Hmong in Asia, and still has a place in the United States. Like many other social and cultural gatherings, alcohol plays a part as a social lubricant.

At a Hmong celebration, such as a graduation, there is a recognition of the support and connectedness of the people gathered. One way this is represented is to have each person tie a string around the wrist of the graduate, while sharing a personal message. A shaman might be present, blessing the occasion.

As with any immigrant population, finances are a concern. Lending circles among the Hmong have helped families share the burden, helping each other in turn.

Have the Hmong been successful in the U.S.? How do you measure success? Economically, they still have a long way to go. In the period after the Great Recession, 2008–2011, a U.S. Census report showed that Asians overall were doing well, with one of the lowest national poverty rates of any race. Yet, the White House Initiative on Asian Americans and Pacific Islanders reported that certain Southeast Asian groups rank among the nation's poorest, with 37.8% of Hmong living in poverty.

On a more personal level, we can see the struggles and adjustments of individual families that carry the Hmong traditions into the new world of the United States. Families are the lifeblood of a culture. Generational differences are significant. Grandparents tend to maintain a firm grasp on the culture they've known from their youth. Parents adapt as they can while serving as the "sandwich" generation. Children go to school and learn English. They juggle to balance a Hmong way-of-life with the familiar domestic environment they encounter day to day.

My father worked hard to pass on his wisdom to his three sons. A man of few words, he effectively used a handful of sayings to communicate his advice. When the appropriate situation presented itself, he would stop, look you in the eye, and solemnly quote the appropriate saying. "Moderation in everything, including moderation." "Don't judge a man until you've walked many moons in his moccasins." My brothers and I became able to recognize a saying with the first word. As a teenager, my own daughter would often interrupt my advice by claiming, "I know what you are going to say, Dad." And she did. I felt honored in a way. She might not follow my advice, but at least she had internalized it.

In the book *The Latehomecomer*, a Hmong grandmother argues with her son about the decision to move from the refugee camp in Thailand to the U.S. She calls her son by his first name, Bee.

"Bee, you cannot leave the camp because I am your mother and I do not want to go to a new land where they will cut into my body when I die. Bee, you cannot leave the camp, because in America a woman controls a man, and I do not want to see my son be the slave of a woman. Bee, you cannot leave the camp, because I do not want to go to live in a new world so far away. ... When I die, my spirit would not be able to find its way across the ocean, to Thailand, to Laos, to the place underneath the platform of my bed, in my old house, where the shirt that carried me into the world was buried."[87]

The family did eventually leave the Thai refugee camp and move to the U.S. But as one of the granddaughters explained, the generations handled the transition differently.

"I saw every day how my mother and father suffered, the long hours they spent trying to be American enough to get into the system so that they could feed us and our dreams. My grandma did not try to be American. She spoke only Hmong. She told stories from long ago. Most importantly, her scent and her clothes remained the same: full of herbs and full of colors, and my childish love for her bloomed into a flowering admiration."[88]

The Hmong New Year is a good place to examine some of the Hmong cultural traditions and how they have fared in the U.S. It is somewhat unusual, falling sometime in December after the work of the harvest is completed. During this celebration, the community takes time to rest and

---

[87] Yang, Kao Kalia. (2008). The Latehomecomer: A Hmong Family Memoir. p. 78-9
[88] Ibid. p.157

engage with each other. The Hmong follow a solar calendar, unlike the Chinese, whose lunar New Year falls in January or February.

As described in *Hmong America*, the traditional Hmong New Year's celebration in Asia is composed of a feast, the ritual of passing from one year to the next and a celebration.[89] No work was allowed during the celebration, so everyone needed to prepare enough food to last until the celebration was done, which would usually last three to five days. Over the course of the year, during the peaceful years, each family would work to raise a hog to butcher during the celebration to share with family and friends. The hog was a measure of the wealth and prosperity of the family, and it was a negative mark for those that had no hog to share.

The New Year's celebration served cultural and religious purposes. Rituals were performed to chase away evil spirits and to honor the spirits of ancestors. Thanks were given for the harvest and ancestors were asked to give the family blessings over the coming year. People blessed each other. People listened to folk songs sung by their sons and daughters and danced. Music was provided in part with a kheng, a bamboo and wooden mouth organ. They played many games, including spear throwing and boxing.

The social value of the feast and surrounding activities went beyond family and community interaction. There was an element of courtship, a chance for young single men and women to meet each other. In Asia, the villages were isolated from each other. Opportunities to meet prospective mates were few.

Ball tossing is an activity which allows a man to show his interest in a woman. During the activities of the New Year, men would observe the women at the gathering, many of them from surrounding villages. If a man found a woman attractive and suitable, he could ask her to toss balls with him, signaling his interest. This also gave the pair some time to get to know each other. To help facilitate the ball tossing, single women might carry cloth balls sewn by someone in the family. Other more direct methods have existed in the past. In one such practice, when a man found a woman he liked, his family would kidnap her and then negotiate with the woman's family for the marriage.

---

[89] Hmong New Year's celebration details from Vang, C.V. (2010) *Hmong America: Reconstructing Community in Diaspora*. University of Illinois Press. p.100-7

Many cultural activities in celebration of the new year have been shared for centuries by a variety of cultures, but the ball tossing activity appears to be unique to the Hmong. Chinese Hmong do not practice it, so evidently ball tossing originated during the Hmong experience in Southeast Asia, as a cultural innovation.

Recognizing the new year is common for most parts of the world. Many cultures gather to celebrate the year end, thinking back over the last year and wishing or praying for success in the year ahead. Many cultures also create ways to accommodate social needs, especially for courtship. Think back to Victorian England where courtship of the privileged had many defined rules, trying to ensure an orderly and successful process that served the needs of parents and their offspring. On New Year's, those with adequate means would invite eligible bachelors to an open house to meet their unmarried daughters. How well that worked I can't say, but I suspect that there was plenty of rule-breaking to get around the rigid system.

Now consider and compare Victorian England to the modern world in a developed country. People have many different options in how they meet, get to know and communicate with others. Recall our discussion regarding online dating. While there might be some defined strategies for finding a spouse or partner, there are many variations and no set path. Birth control has been a game-changer, altering previous patterns of male/female behavior. Overall, culturally orchestrated personal interactions have lost their importance in many places of the world.

It's ironic that with the increase of possibilities and communication paths, many people still feel lonely. In various places the marriage rate has fallen, as singles put off marriage until later in life or decide against it. This situation reflects what we have discussed, a new world of transparency, abundant choices, and instability that translates into a loose collection of lifestyles and individual decision-makers.

The cultural traditions of the Hmong New Year have been impacted by their new location in the U.S. As you can imagine, when Hmong communities in the U.S. were new, putting together a suitable and culturally adequate New Year celebration was difficult. With many Hmong relocating to larger cities, their very lifestyle was altered and the thought of raising a pig for the New Year was unrealistic. Just finding a way to bring multiple families together in an outdoor celebration was challenging, especially in a place like Minnesota in the winter.

As the Hmong population grew and social service agencies were developed, people looked to them for assistance. Social service agencies struggled and argued about how to proceed. At times there was either an ignorance of the traditions, or a diverse collection of Southeast Asians with different ideas on goals and paths to follow. In Minnesota, the decision to merge the New Year celebration with the non-Hmong Lao community was not universally accepted by either community. Because of differences, including the different dates of the New Year for each group, the Hmong community ended up on their own.

As parents did what they could to translate the traditions into a new context, there emerged intergenerational conflict. Older Hmong longed for the true traditions and did not consider newer activities, such as beauty contests, to be authentic. The compromises diminished the emotional connection. The American experience broadened the expressions of art, music, and dance. Inevitably, commercialism creeped into the celebration, to the dismay of many.

In 2019 in Minnesota, the 41st annual Minnesota Hmong New Year was a two-day event held in a large facility in St. Paul, hosted by United Hmong Family, Inc. It was a celebration that "highlighted traditional Hmong dance, music, crafts, vendors and more." There was a dance and singing competition. Even more relevant to our discussion, there was an essay contest in 2020 with a theme of embracing the present and inspiring future generations: "Each writer is tasked with laying out what the present looks like today -- by examining how far we have come as a community and expounding on some of the challenges still facing the Hmong community and the works that still lie ahead. ... The essay should conclude by positing how EMBRACING combined with INSPIRING can serve to unify and empower the Hmong community."

The essay was an attempt to articulate how to "unify and empower the Hmong community." It's an admirable goal, but challenging. While outsiders might look at Hmong people with no differentiation, that's not the reality. Hmong come from different countries and each person belongs to his own generation. If we use four different countries and three different generations, that's 12 different categories on those attributes alone. We could add religion as a factor, as some of the resettled Hmong accepted Christianity from their sponsors. People also belong to different clans.

Each clan is unique in how it performs Hmong rites and rituals. In 2005, to create a stronger bond among the Hmong, a pamphlet called, "Hmong Traditional Culture Procedural Guide" was created by one of the leaders with the idea of standardizing Hmong ritual behavior. For example, one of the guidelines was to cap the bride prices at $5,000. These and other rules were not well received as they took the negotiating power and decision-making out of the hands of the clan leaders.

I question if there are enough common attributes and goals among this group to motivate individuals to work together. The Hmong are creating a new identity in the U.S. based on a shared past, a common ancestry, and defining struggles. Yet a free society in a diverse setting gives people more choices. If a culture needs to change (kidnapping is no longer an option), new shared behaviors will need to emerge, as ball-tossing did in Asia.

Again, from *Hmong America*: "One [perspective] is that current performances have abandoned Hmong culture and traditions, attributed both to the borrowing of other cultures' arts and to the lack of interest in traditional activities."[90]

Hmong Funerals

How people respond to death is another enlightening cultural element. A traditional Hmong funeral is days long and reflects many different cultural beliefs. The associated cultural practices carried out in China and Laos needed some adjusting to work in the U.S.

Traditional Hmong funerals would last seven days, but Hmong funerals in the U.S. are typically three to four days long, often starting on Friday and concluding with the burial on Monday. The funeral service carries on for 24 hours a day. A special bamboo instrument called a qeej is played along with drums. Hmong-specific funeral homes have sprung up to accommodate the special requirements.[91]

---

[90] Vang, C.V. (2010) *Hmong America: Reconstructing Community in Diaspora.* University of Illinois Press. p.105

[91] Hmong funeral practices from Funeralwise. (2022). Hmong Funeral Service Rituals. *Funeralwise.* http://funeralwise.com/customs/hmong/

Hmong beliefs are animistic. After death, a person's soul is said to reincarnate into a different spiritual form. There are beliefs about the journey of the spirit after death. One such belief is that each family needs a son to guide the spirit back to the other world. A related cultural practice is to place a chicken near the head of the deceased to provide a meal for the journey. Many of the participants at the funeral will fold paper into "money boats" to sail along with the spirit and provide wealth. Speaking of wealth, it is also expected that many visitors to the funeral will donate money to offset the cost of the funeral and to support the family.

As noted, some Hmong have adopted Christianity. This has resulted in a new mix of traditional Hmong and Christian practices. Christian Hmong families might still use the same Hmong funeral homes and many of the funerals also last three to four days. But the music, rituals and beliefs are different. As one would expect, the transition of some Hmong people to Christianity and the resulting changes to the traditional funeral have created some friction. Adding to that, Hmong churches tend to be split by clan.

What used to be small, isolated, homogeneous clans in Asia are now thrown together in a new environment. Their differences are highlighted as they attempt to form a larger community that can gain enough scale in a foreign land to exercise self-determination. Time is working against them as the new generations begin to assimilate into the prevailing culture and seek other goals.

Hmong culture survived the migration to Southeast Asia, preserving and adding to cultural beliefs and traditions. In the next migration, many Hmong also made lives for themselves in the U.S. They have banded together and adapted their traditions. But the U.S. presents different challenges. They are no longer isolated, they have transparent access to information through digital means, and they have expanding choices on how to live. These conditions could mean that Hmong cultural life in this new world might eventually become a shadow of the past, like so many other cultures.

Remember the Lutheran sponsors we mentioned? Many of those immigrants have been in the U.S. for a couple of generations. One tradition that the older generations try to maintain is the holiday consumption of lutefisk. It's a whitefish soaked in lye, rendering it into a jelly-like form that is best eaten with a mountain of gravy. Cultural comfort food?

Those who remain in the Nordic countries, from where this practice came, have happily relegated this meal to the past. Having sampled lutefisk, I'll call that cultural progress.

Part III
A Brighter Future

Chapter 13

Making our Way

I would like to close with my thoughts on how we as a society might move forward. At the most basic and simplistic level, people need love. But as we discussed earlier, history has shown that love and associated relationships absolutely need a structure and patterns of behavior to guide their complicated dance of caring interaction.

In Part II of this book, I tried to paint a picture of paths forward using the global interviews as an inspiration and framework. When we abandon the many assumptions that would lead us astray and instead focus on our shared human nature, we can approach each new person with more confidence. When we focus on our commonality, our pathway widens to allow us to walk side-by-side. As we walk together, we begin to learn and respect the history and values that make each person unique. The interviews themselves provided examples of how people in different circumstances have formed and followed their own pathways.

Here in Part III, we'll look at the big picture, the macro environment. You'll learn what I believe the future holds for our cultures, and how we might consider providing support and direction.

There is an essential truth that seems to be slipping away from us as we become more technology-enabled and seek perfection. Stripping away all our cultural foundation and human nature in pursuit of an idealized, stylized self is destined for failure. It's ironic that at the same time our world gets better and better at creating flawless, artificial celebrities, filtering out their smallest imperfections, the electronic world is exposing people's humanness, never forgetting their broken past, and failing to block out today's bullies. The truth lies somewhere in between. The answer is not to totally dismiss our cultures and build an individual, independent bubble of reality, nor is it to return to a world where an all-encompassing cultural framework directs our every move. The environmental shifts we've covered require something refreshing: a new balance of culture and personal pathways that acknowledges the authenticity of our human nature and rejects practices that break our moral code.

Balance means that you are in control. You know the tradeoffs of sticking to cultural precedents. You understand the effort to supplement the past with new ideas and patterns. You've established your identities in a way that allows you to interact with people who are different without a feeling of defensiveness. You confidently face diversity with an understanding of our commonality, our shared human nature.

The Future

I've presented some societal and technical forces that are influencing our pathways. Consider where we are headed. What has occurred more frequently over the course of human existence, equality or imbalance? Each section of the world, whether it be a country, business, or school, tends to consist of the "haves" and "have nots." With this upsetting of the traditional cultural infrastructure, I see the possibility of three general segments emerging:

- People looking for guidance and stability in a world where former preset patterns of behavior are no longer sustainable: the "have nots."
- People with resilient patterns of behavior and additional resources who are better able to make sense of new inputs and secure their place in the world: the "haves."
- People who focus on taking advantage of shifts, gaps, and trends and try to alter them for their own benefit: the opportunists.

The new normal will be a world where holistic cultures will lose their advantage as a road map for life. As you've seen throughout history, certain people will use this situation to their advantage. They will try to control the messaging. There will be many people acting as individuals, latching on to values as they see fit, and loosely associating with a pathway when it is advantageous to do so. Barriers will continue to isolate people and confine them within a level of the hierarchy.

Many of the individual voices will tend to reinforce the status quo rather than promote more diversity. Why? Because to resist the standard would be too costly. As we noted before, the permanence of the public record has reached new heights. Anything captured digitally is now discoverable for your lifetime and beyond. We have seen this phenomenon play out multiple times, as texts or pictures from years ago surface and have profound effects on careers and reputations. Ironically, this newfound visibility and monitoring of your communication history could produce a chilling effect on contrary opinions. No doubt you have witnessed how social media can be weaponized. When a wave of influencers decides what words, thoughts, and actions are acceptable or not, and selectively targets people for their past behavior, people take notice.

The following two statements are my guiding principles for dealing with this global cultural transformation.

- Organic, grassroots cultures are the best cultures for people because they are the most relevant and compatible with human nature, but they need support and oversight. They will provide a supporting role to individual pathways, rather than a dominant one.

- In contrast, the shaping of culture by institutions will always be influenced and skewed by the goals of the institution. They can't be allowed to dominate the cultural landscape.

My recommendations:

- Think twice about trying to resurrect broad-based traditional cultures through intervention. They are struggling because they

197

are incompatible with current conditions, and they will likely continue to fail.

- By working together with diverse people on shared goals, we can be part of a more sustainable form of grassroots culture. Your experience and intuition will serve as the best means to reconstitute culture.
- Don't expect these new forms of culture to conform to all your intellectual ideals. Cultures are shaped by values which are inevitably compromised by reality and then bundled into an acceptable whole.
- Realize that people need structure and will continue to classify and categorize themselves and others. For the good of the world, we will need to do this in a constructive fashion, guided by a moral compass that accounts for human capabilities and limitations. People can be considered different and unique, but not inferior or superior.

Tools

In addition to forming your individual pathways, I hope you will be part of the grassroots human interaction to define sustainable shared pathways. Please accept and support these new pathways within the diverse community, and work to improve them. You will need these new forms to counter-balance the institutional cultures governed by the powerful. Finally, be a voice of reason to counter the destructive forces and support a moral compass.

Here's another recommendation: empathy. Why is empathy so important? Because we all need empathy to deal with what lies ahead.

Empathy: The psychological identification with or vicarious experiencing of the feelings, thoughts, or attitudes of another.

Empathy will require opening your life to others and taking risks. The resulting richness of life can be well worth it. Seek and share knowledge. Use it to continuously refine your world view and your cultural mind-map.[92] Try learning another language, tutoring kids from a different neighborhood, or visiting a new church. I recommend subscribing to Worldcrunch, a truly international daily newsletter.

For the future, my hope is that smaller and more adaptable cultures will help carry people through their personal challenges. As we discussed in the Identity chapter, people are developing multiple ways of handling various roles. In a similar way, future cultures could take different forms, perhaps operating at a more generalized level. A handful of universal cultural vectors (love, justice, etc.) will continue. Inevitably, there will also be many people caught between worlds and without a community to which they can belong. A returning veteran. An immigrant. An awkward teenager.

As hard as people try, forming broad stereotypes of the people outside of their own identity group will get harder and more unreliable. Unlike movie dramas, the world is not made up of pure good guys and bad guys. With an abundance of information, my hope is that more people will realize this. There will always be an "us" and "them," but the "them" will not be a homogeneous and stagnant "other," and it never was. The best approach to a rewarding relationship is to focus on what we share and to understand and appreciate each individual person and their situation. Empathy is the means to that end.

Technology can be supportive. I applaud the current use of artificial reality (AR) to help people better understand the perspective and challenges of those with disabilities. What a creative idea, but why stop there? Could we mold an experience in AR that would help people understand what it's like to live in poverty, be a single parent, or suffer from prejudice?

Humans all have the potential for empathy. When people use it well, it will serve as a shock absorber between the evolving cultures and the people lost among them. It's not just a matter of being nice. Without a healthy dose of empathy, people could be headed for conflict through global misunderstandings.

In engineering, there is a specification called tolerance, which allows for variation. Different applications call for different levels of tolerance

---

[92] Personally, I have a lot of room for improvement in showing empathy. I'm working on it.

(also called forgiveness). In human life, many faiths provide a path for forgiveness. Yet somehow forgiveness is elusive in a world that is beginning to reject cultural social contracts and spiritual formulas. In such a world, how can forgiveness be achieved?

My ultimate vision is to move away from a world where groups of people are dismissed with a stereotype to a world where empathy is extended to individuals.

Organizational Intervention

My concern: The possibility exists that traditional culture, in its transitional state, will be outmatched by the power of incumbent institutions that will drive behavior to suit their needs. Without intervention, the retreat of culture could leave a void in the lives of many people. The void will leave people more on their own to deal with societal challenges and manipulative forces, a potential mental health issue.

Could we be pro-active?

- Remember the battle over sex education in schools? People resisted. They seemed to think that kids would figure it all out naturally and that sex education would be an overreach by the state. A concerted effort could now be made to teach people how to form their individual pathways and deal with cultural conflict. Multicultural competence is a requirement for thriving in our new world. It doesn't all come naturally. People will also need help living with new levels of ambiguity and complexity.

- With help from sociologists, the mental health community is best positioned to understand the essential foundations of healthy cultures and individual pathways. Just as people are learning the essentials of healthy one-on-one relationships, people must also be made aware of the requirements of productive group interaction. This can't be left to chance. As new forms of culture emerge from the interactions of people, we can't afford to perpetuate racism, sexism, and fear-based thinking. These new forms of culture must be capable of bringing diverse people together based on respect and common values.

- The educational community is best positioned to communicate and teach these values to a new generation. This alone will not create a culture — that is not the intent, but it will give worthy guidance. For this to work, the mental health and educational communities must unselfishly pursue what is best for all.
- The greatest risk will be to do nothing. Without action, the reconstitution of culture will leave a void that will be filled by those with selfish intentions and new forms of culture that could perpetuate the old mistakes.
- As with any change to the status quo, there will be resistance.

On our own, we can't save or create a broadly shared culture. But having read this book, I hope that you are better prepared for what is coming, not because it provides all the answers, but because it gives you a chance to consider your response to the new realities. If I've been successful, you'll be in a better position to help yourself and others bridge the gaps and chart a course in the times ahead. Largely due to the kind and supportive people I have met, I have been able to realize hope, joy, and productivity in diversity. I wish the same for all.

Finally, don't rely on intelligence and logic alone. We all need relationships and meaning in our lives, and that is best accomplished in a nurturing and supportive world that recognizes our unique humanity. Unleash your power of empathy to counter the divisiveness. Realize joy in our diversity. Make your way.

Bibliography

Ai Weiwei (Director). (2017). *Human Flow* [Film]. Amazon Studios

Anderson, M., Vogels, E. A., & Turner, E. (2020, February 6). The Virtues and Downsides of Online Dating. *Pew Research Center.* https://www.pewresearch.org/internet/2020/02/06/the-virtues-and-downsides-of-online-dating/

Boynton, Robert S. (2016). *The Invitation-only Zone: The true story of North Korea's abduction project.* Farrar, Straus, and Giroux

Bureau of Labor Statistics News Release. (2021, August 31). U.S. Department of Labor. https://www.bls.gov/news.release/pdf/nlsoy.pdf

Burt, Chris. (2019, April 29). Heathrow curb-to-gate biometrics said to be world's biggest single deployment. *Biometrics Research Group, Inc.* https://www.biometricupdate.com/201904/heathrow-curb-to-gate-biometrics-said-to-be-worlds-biggest-single-deployment

Carter, Rita. (2008). *Multiplicity: The New Science of Personality, Identity, and the Self.* Little, Brown, and Company

Cattane N, Rossi R, Lanfredi M, Cattaneo A. (2017). Borderline personality disorder and childhood trauma: exploring the affected biological systems and mechanisms. *BMC Psychiatry.* 2017 Jun 15;17(1):221. doi: 10.1186/s12888-017-1383-2. PMID: 28619017; PMCID: PMC5472954.

CDC WONDER, Multiple Cause of Death Files. (2019). America's Health Rankings analysis of CDC WONDER, Multiple Cause of Death Files, United Health Foundation, AmericasHealthRankings.org, accessed 2022.

Bibliography

Chang, Jung. (2013). *Empress Dowager Cixi: The Concubine Who Launched Modern China*. Alfred A. Knopf

Collier, Paul. (2018). *The Future of Capitalism: Facing the New Anxieties*. HarperCollins

Davidson, John. (2019, June 18). How Should We Think About Declining Denominational Numbers? *Christianity Today*

De Mente, Boyé Lafayette. (2004) *Korean Business Etiquette*. Tuttle Publishing

De Mente, Boyé Lafayette. (2012). *Korean Mind: Understanding Contemporary Korean Culture*. Tuttle Publishing

Demick, Barbara. (2010). *Nothing to Envy: Ordinary Lives in North Korea*. Spiegel & Grau

Diamond, Jared. (1997). *Guns, Germs, and Steel: The Fates of Human Societies*. W. W. Norton and Company

Dinets, Vladimir. (2016). *Wildlife Spectacles: Mass Migrations, Mating Rituals, and Other Fascinating Animal Behaviors*. Timber Press

Dobbin, F., Kalev, A., & Kelly, E. (2007). Diversity management in corporate America. *Contexts*, 6(4), 21-27.

Ebadi, Shirin. (2016). *Until We are Free: My Fight for Human Rights in Iran*. Random House

Esipova, N., Pugliese, A., & Ray, J. (2013, May 15). 381 Million Adults Worldwide Migrate Within Countries. *Gallup*. https://news.gallup.com/poll/162488/381-million-adults-worldwide-migrate-within-countries.aspx

Euromonitor International. (2018). Future of the Family. *Euromonitor International.* Retrieved June 1, 2022 from https://go.euromonitor.com/white-paper-households-2019-future_of_the_family.html

Fadiman, Anne. (1997). *The Spirit Catches You and You Fall Down: A Hmong Child, Her American Doctors, and the Collision of Two Cultures.* Farrar, Straus, and Giroux

Fitzgerald, F. Scott. (1945). *The Crack-Up.* New Directions. p. 69

Fragile States Index. (2022). *The Fund for Peace.* https://fragilestatesindex.org/global-data/

Freud, Sigmund. (1989). *The Freud Reader.* W. W. Norton & Company

Funeralwise. (2022). Hmong Funeral Service Rituals. *Funeralwise.* http://funeralwise.com/customs/hmong/

GaijinPot (2019). Kawasaki Halloween Parade. *GPlusMedia.* https://travel.gaijinpot.com/kawasaki-halloween-parade/

Gascoigne, Bamber. (2003). *The Dynasties of China: A History.* Carroll & Graf Publishers

Gladwell, Malcolm. (2019). *Talking to Strangers: What We Should Know about the People We Don't Know.* Little, Brown, and Company

Gordon, Stewart. (2008). *When Asia was the World.* Da Capo Press

Ha, Lan & Angus, Alison. (2021, March 15). New Strategies to Engage Millennials and Generation Z in Times of Uncertainty. *Euromonitor.* https://www.euromonitor.com/article/new-strategies-to-engage-millennials-and-generation-z-in-times-of-uncertainty

Bibliography

Her, Vincent K., & Buley-Meissner, Mary Louise (Eds.). (2012). *Hmong and American: From Refugees to Citizens*. Minnesota Historical Society Press

Holt, Daniel D. & Holt, Grace Massey. (1988). *Korean at a Glance*. Barron's Educational Series, Inc.

Hong, Euny. (2014). *The Birth of Korean Cool*. Picador

Huie, Wing Young. (2018). *Chinese-ness*. Minnesota Historical Society Press

Huey Lewis and the News. (1986). Hip to be Square [Song]. On *Fore!*

Kamali, Mohammad Hashim. (2008). *Shari'ah Law: An Introduction*. Oneworld Publications

Kang, Chol-hwan & Rigoulot, Pierre. (2001). *The Aquariums of Pyongyang: Ten Years in the North Korean Gulag*. Basic Books

Kim, Suki. (2014). *Without You, There Is No Us: My Time with the Sons of North Korea's Elite*. Crown Publishers

King, Charles. (2019). *Gods of the Upper Air*. Doubleday

Kirby, Jen. (2020, Feb 24). *Syria's worst humanitarian catastrophe in it 9-year civil war is now unfolding*. Vox. https://www.vox.com/2020/2/24/21142307/idlib-syria-civil-war-assad-russia-turkey

Kleinman, Alexis. (2013, March 29). *How The Red Equal Sign Took Over Facebook, According To Facebook's Own Data*. Huffpost. https://www.huffpost.com/entry/red-equal-sign-facebook_n_2980489

Lee, Erika. (2015). *The Making of Asian America: A History.* Simon & Schuster

Lewis, Richard D. (2006). *When Cultures Collide: Leading across cultures.* Nicolas Brealey International

Livingston, Gretchen. (2018, April 25). The Changing Profile of Unmarried Parents. *Pew Research Center.* https://www.pewresearch.org/social-trends/2018/04/25/the-changing-profile-of-unmarried-parents/

Majd, Hooman. (2013). *The Ministry of Guidance invites you to NOT STAY.* Doubleday

Manyika, James, Silberg, Jake, & Presten, Brittany. (2019, October 25). What Do We Do About the Biases in AI. *Harvard Business Review* https://hbr.org/2019/10/what-do-we-do-about-the-biases-in-ai

Maslow, A. H. (1954) *Motivation and Personality* (1st ed.). Harper

Moisi, Dominique. (2010). *The Geopolitics of Emotion: How Cultures of Fear, Humiliation, and Hope are reshaping the World.* Anchor Books

Moseley, Christopher (Ed.). (2010). *Atlas of the World's Languages in Danger.* UNESCO Publishing

National People's Congress (NPC) of the People's Republic of China. (English version available 2006). China Constitution. *General Office of the NPC of the People's Republic of China.* http://www.npc.gov.cn/zgrdw/englishnpc/Constitution/node_2825.htm

Navai, Ramita. (2014). *City of Lies: Love, Sex, Death and the Search for Truth in Tehran.* PublicAffairs

Bibliography

News China. (Aug 2016). Netizenwatch: Nerd Lovers. *China Newsweek Corporation*

News China. (Dec 2019). Netizenwatch: Village Ban on Funeral Gowns Quickly Killed. *China Newsweek Corporation*

News China. (Aug 2016). Netizenwatch: Watermelon Warriors. *China Newsweek Corporation*

Ngai, Mae. (2022). *The Chinese Question: The Gold Rushes, Chinese Migration, and Global Politics.* W. W. Norton and Company

Nisbett, Richard E. (2003). *The Geography of Thought.* Free Press

Nordell, Jessica. (2021). *The End of Bias: A Beginning.* Metropolitan Books, Henry Holt and Company

Number of international tourist arrivals worldwide from 1950 to 2021 (2022) *Statista.* https://news.gallup.com/poll/162488/381-million-adults-worldwide-migrate-within-countries.aspx

Open Doors. (2018). *2018 Open Doors Report on International Educational Exchange.* Institute of International Education and U.S. Department of State's Bureau of Educational and Cultural Affairs. https://studyinthestates.dhs.gov/2018/11/open-doors-report-record-high-number-international-students#:~:text=The%20Open%20Doors%20Report%20for,b illion%20to%20the%20U.S.%20economy.

Pakula, Hannah. (2009). *The Last Empress: Madame Chiang Kai-shek and the birth of modern China.* Simon and Schuster Paperbacks

Palgrave Macmillan (Ed.). (2020). *The Statesman's Yearbook 2020: The Politics, Cultures and Economies of the World,* Palgrave Macmillan

Park, Yeonmi. (2015). *In Order to Live: A North Korean Girl's Journey to Freedom.* Penguin Random House

Pew Research Center. (2018, February 28). *Origins and Destinations of the World's Migrants, 1990-2017.* https://www.pewresearch.org/global/interactives/global-migrant-stocks-map/

Pulse of Asia. (2019). How do Asians celebrate Christmas? *1-StopAsia.* https://www.1stopasia.com/blog/how-do-asians-celebrate-christmas/

Ramakrishnan, Karthick & Ahmad, Farah Z. (2014, September) *State of Asian Americans and Pacific Islanders Series: A Multifaceted Portrait of a Growing Population.* Center for American Progress – AAPI Data

Rhie, Won-bok. (2002). *Korea Unmasked: In search of the country, the society, and the people.* Gimm International, Inc.

Rich, Motoko. (2019, December 17). Dying Japan Town lives on via dolls. *New York Times*

Ropp, Paul S. (2010). *China in World History.* Oxford University Press

Satell, Greg. (2015, May 1). The Science of Patterns. *Forbes*

Secor, Laura. (2016). *Children of Paradise: The Struggle for the Soul of Iran.* Riverhead Books

Scheer, Robert. (2015). *They know Everything about You.* Nation Books

Snyder, S. A. (2021) The two Koreas. *Foreign Policy Association: Great Decisions*

Starr, John Bryan. (2010) *Understanding China: A Guide to China's Economy, History, and Political Culture.* Hill and Wang

Bibliography

Storr, Will. (2018) *Selfie: How We Became So Self-Obsessed and What It's Doing to Us.* Abrams Press

Takada, Noriko & Lampkin, Rita L. (1997). *The Japanese Way: Aspects of Behavior, Attitudes, and Customs of the Japanese.* The McGraw-Hill Companies, Inc.

The Atlanta Journal-Constitution. (June 26, 2015). Georgia Congressman John Lewis reacts to gay marriage ruling. https://www.ajc.com/blog/news/georgia-congressman-john-lewis-reacts-gay-marriage-ruling/XTUyxBIQerIoWjw98ftebK/

The Economist. (May 3, 2007). The World goes to Town. *The Economist Newspaper.* https://www.economist.com/special-report/2007/05/03/the-world-goes-to-town

Treuer, Anton. (2021). *The Cultural Toolbox: Traditional Ojibwe Living in the Modern World.* Minnesota Historical Society Press.

TRIANGLE in ASEAN Quarterly Briefing Note. (2021). *International Labour Organization.* https://www.ilo.org/wcmsp5/groups/public/---asia/---ro-bangkok/documents/genericdocument/wcms_735109.pdf

Tsai, Chih-Hao. (1996). *Frequency and Stroke Counts of Chinese Characters.* Chih-Hao Tsai Technology Page, http://technology.chtsai.org/charfreq/

Tschentscher, A. (Ed.). (2013). *German Constitution in English.* International Constitutional Law (ICL). http://www.servat.unibe.ch/icl/gm00000_.html

Turino, Thomas. (2004). *Identity and the Arts in Diaspora Communities.* Harmonie Park Press

Vallet, Elisabeth. (2022, March 2). The World Is Witnessing a Rapid Proliferation of Border Walls. *Migration Policy Institute.*

https://www.migrationpolicy.org/article/rapid-proliferation-number-border-walls

Vang, Chia Youyee. (2010). *Hmong America: Reconstructing Community in Diaspora.* University of Illinois Press

Wang, Cheng-Tong Lir & Schofer, Evan. (Dec 2018) *Coming out of the penumbras: World culture and cross-national variation in divorce rates* (Social Forces, Volume 97, Issue 2, December 2018, Pages 675–704). Oxford University Press. https://doi.org/10.1093/sf/soy070

Weatherford, Jack. (2004). *Genghis Khan and the making of the Modern World.* Three Rivers Press

Wong, Theresa, Yeoh, Brenda S. A., Graham, Elspeth F. & Teo, Peggy. (2004, January/February). Spaces of silence: single parenthood and the 'normal family 'in Singapore. *Population, Space, and Place,* Volume10, Issue1. Pages 43-58

Woodhams, Samuel, & Migliano, Simon. (Jun 23, 2022). Government Internet Shutdowns Have Cost Over $26 Billion Since 2019. *TOP10VPN.* https://www.top10vpn.com/research/cost-of-internet-shutdowns/

Working the Flame. (Sep 2021). Most Common Jobs in the 1800s. https://workingtheflame.com/common-jobs-in-the-1800s/

World Health Organization. (2018). LIVE LIFE: Preventing Suicide. *Department of Mental Health and Substance Abuse, World Health Organization* https://cdn.who.int/media/docs/default-source/mental-health/suicide/live-life-brochure.pdf?sfvrsn=6ea28a12_2&download=true

Wu, Hao (Director). (2018). *People's Republic of Desire* [Film]

Bibliography

Wuthnow, Robert. (2018). *The Left Behind: Decline and Rage in Rural America*. Princeton University Press

Xinhua News Agency. (Jan 3, 2020). Across China: E-commerce a fast track to prosperity for poor mountainous areas. *China Economic Information Service*

Xue, Xinran. (2009). *China Witness*. Pantheon Books

Yang, Kao Kalia. (2008). *The Latehomecomer: A Hmong Family Memoir*. Coffee House Press

Yi, Ziyi. (Nov 2019). Sex, Lips, and Videotape. *News China, China Newsweek Corporation*

Yu, Hua. (2011). *China in Ten Words*. Pantheon Books

Zhang, Y. & Van Hook, J. (2009). Marital Dissolution Among Interracial Couples. *Journal of Marriage and Family*, vol. 71, no. 1. https://onlinelibrary.wiley.com/doi/abs/10.1111/j.1741-3737.2008.00582.x

Zhisui, Dr. Li. (1994). *The Private Life of Chairman Mao: the memoirs of Mao's personal physician*. Random House, Inc.

Zuckerman, Ethan. (2013). *Rewire: Digital Cosmopolitans in the Age of Connection*. W. W. Norton and Company

Acknowledgements

I want to acknowledge the global participants that came to the U.S. for a month-long program in 2007 and opened my eyes to the richness, collaboration, and creativity of diverse cultures. From that point on, there was no turning back.

Thanks to all who provided support and feedback through the creation and production of this book, especially my family. Jan provided patient reading and feedback on all my drafts. The kind support of Jan, Emily, and Adam kept me going.

Steve Bornhoft, with his lifelong professional writing experience, has been a generous mentor, guide, and inspiration. I came to him with an idea and through his considerate coaching, I found my voice. His editing brought the writing to a new level. This book would not have been possible without him.

I am deeply grateful to those I have interviewed or peppered endlessly with questions. Many people have blessed me with fascinating experiences and stories. Thank you for opening your lives. I hope that despite my many missteps my interaction with you has borne fruit.

Thanks to 3M and to the University of Minnesota whose MOT master's degree program included an international residency that planted a seed.

我非常感谢我的中文老师和同学给我带来学习中文的快乐和文化领悟。

Afterword

In 1999, I was in the second year of a graduate program at the University of Minnesota with a goal to augment my degree in sociology with a master's degree in management of technology. Little did I know that this educational mix concerning people and technology would prove both invaluable and insufficient in the years ahead. In this, our final semester, our class would travel to Shanghai and Singapore to gain an international perspective.

Our graduate class was a rather diverse group, and all of us had worked a few years after graduating college. Our class was organized into small study groups. If religious diversity is any sign of an effective team, my small group of five was well positioned. Mormon, Jewish, Islamic and Christian faiths were all represented.

So, it was with some degree of naive confidence that we started our journey to Asia. Every day in Shanghai was a revelation:

In one of our first lectures, I was intimidated as I heard a China official claim China's right to Taiwan and its willingness to militarily defend that right against any country, including the U.S. An odd welcome.

I learned how companies like Medtronic had difficulty breaking into China because the older generation was not willing to spend precious resources on their health over the needs of their children.

We toured a gigantic state-owned Enterprise (SOE) facility that appeared to be totally automated until the lunch period ended, and scores of workers returned. Our impression of the inefficiency of SOEs was reconfirmed.

After a few days in Shanghai, I felt comfortable asking my own question to a Chinese government authority. We were staying at what was then the outskirts of the booming city. Outside our hotel was the unfinished skeleton of a freeway overpass with exit and entrance ramps that ended in midair.

It was this scene that led to my ill-conceived question at one of our daily Shanghai lectures. "We are staying at a hotel and outside the hotel there is an unfinished freeway intersection," I said. "During our stay, we have not noticed any work getting done. What might be holding up the work? Is there a shortage of resources or labor?"

What I thought to be a reasonable question clearly insulted our speaker. "We have no shortages of any material here and our supply of labor is unlimited," he said.

The lecture was on a Friday. A day later, the class noticed that the construction site teemed with workers and production was in full swing. The American students (one in particular) were being taught a lesson.

Our next destination was Singapore. On arrival, we received a tour and presentation from a group representing business opportunities in the squeaky-clean city-state. The tour included a couple of state-of-the-art manufacturing facilities. Our hosts had just shared their strategy of expanding Singapore's success as a shipping hub to encompass a new global digital hub.

In conversation with Singapore residents, I mustered the courage to suggest that Singapore "use all of the people available to meet their goals." It was a thinly veiled plea to loosen gender-based restrictions that I had witnessed. In turn, I was told that all kinds of people were fairly represented in the workforce. As the meeting broke up, a classmate whispered to me that my input was not received warmly. As our hosts mingled with the class after the discussion, looking for potential candidates for employment, I was ignored despite my digital background.

As part of the pre-trip briefing for the trip and from friends, I had heard of the strict governmental control in Singapore directed by what seems to be a secretive group of leaders. In terms of economy and standard of living, the leaders have been tremendously successful. In terms of fostering creative thinking, not so much. During our visit, we noted the government-funded public-service displays on the subway walls encouraging new perspectives and creative thought. Another shortcoming of the population, from the perspective of the city-state's strategy, is the lack of marriages and children. One tactic to get romance kickstarted and consummated in marriage was the promotion of themed cruises, targeting singles.

Based on these interactions in our brief visit, it would be easy for this group of students to come to some generalized and superficial conclusions about China and Singapore. We certainly did. As humans, we:

- Prefer to capture our experiences in crisp, tidy explanations.
- Favor conclusions that are consistent with our already established beliefs.
- Seek answers that are personally beneficial.

Had my interaction with Asia and other international locations ended with this trip, I would probably still be harboring many of these quickly formed misconceptions and passing them on to others. As it happened, the next 20 years were filled with working directly with people from many countries in multiple global roles. Those early ideas were challenged, and I was forced to change my world views. I had no globally encompassing cultural pathway to follow. I was on my own.

That's the same process that is chipping away at the existing cultures of the world. Beliefs are becoming outdated as evidence proves them wrong. Beliefs become incongruous as people no longer conform to group expectations and elect to take new options. Beliefs are deemed harmful when we recognize how they categorize and pit people against each other. All this cultural erosion is fueled by a new level of transparency that is enabled by technology.

As I've shared in this book, I believe that we are headed to a new era in which many people will begin to shed their inflexible cultural roadmaps, not necessarily because they want to, but because traditional culture can no longer serve the role it has held for centuries. Without that onramp to a well-defined cultural pathway, individuals will need to manage their own navigation through life, something many of us could be ill-prepared to do.

Given the dysfunctional experience we've had with cult figures, political parties, and social influencers rushing to fill the cultural gap with questionable motives, I believe that a recognition of the issue and healthy proactive alternatives are vital.

Let's make a way, a better way, to support the successful navigation of our personal and collective journeys in our wonderfully diverse world.

About the Author

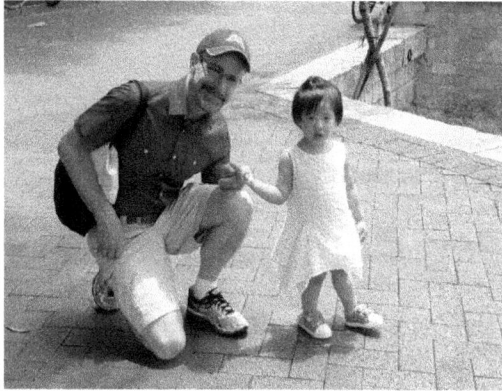

Mark Bornhoft

While research and education shape his conclusions, Mark Bornhoft has learned his most cherished lessons from a wide range of talented people from across the world.

As a senior e-transformation leader at a global Fortune 500 company, he produced proprietary studies on the complexities of global cross-country collaboration. With this book, 12 Voices, he invites you to hear from citizens of the global cultural landscape, explore commentary, and come to your own conclusions.

As you might expect, Mark Bornhoft's personal life reflects a strong interest in diverse cultures and social issues. His volunteer work includes tutoring immigrant kids and providing support to people in ICE detention. He has a degree in sociology from Gustavus Adolphus College and a master's in management of technology from the University of Minnesota.

Mark lives with his family in Minnesota. (He is pictured above with his friends' daughter in Singapore.)

www.ingramcontent.com/pod-product-compliance
Lightning Source LLC
Chambersburg PA
CBHW070802280326
41934CB00012B/3028